IMMORTAL

BREATH OF

CHRIST

Alma Nahra Aumen-el

Jeffrey Scott Pears

Published by Jeffrey Scott Pears

Print Edition 1, 2020

U.S. Copyright Office Number: TXU002150044

ISBN: 978-0-578-55596-6

The author of this book does not dispense medical advice or prescribe the use of any technique as a form of treatment for physical or medical problems without the advice of a physician, either directly or indirectly. The intent of the author is only to offer information of a general nature to help you in your quest for living the life you desire to live. In the event you use any of the information in this book for yourself, which is your constitutional right, the author and the publisher assume no responsibility for your actions.

On the cover: The Immortal Breath of Christ (Alma Nahra Aumen-el) whereas in Aramaic to English translation: Alma means "Eternal," Nahra means "Breath," and Aumen-el (later pronounced Emmanuel or Immanuel) means "God is with us."

IMMORTAL
BREATH OF
CHRIST

Alma Nahra Aumen-el

Jeffrey Scott Pears

ACKNOWLEDGMENTS

Deepest gratitude to:

Jesus the Christ, Swami Krishnananda of The Divine Life Society, Goswami Kriyananda of the Temple of Kriya Yoga, Robert Moss, John White, Kwan Yin, St. John of the Cross, St. Teresa of Avila, the Maharishi and others who have contributed to the birthing of this book including my good friends Jim Matthews, Joe Meboe, Cynthia Moore, my family of Patti, Jacob and Sarah, Jessica and Trent, Steve, Kira, Penny and Jerome, Barbara, Faye, and my grandchildren Oliver, Parker and Rowan.

NOTE: This book was written by an interfaith hospice-chaplain about his personal metaphysical experiences, spiritual revelations, and inner-life communication with the Divine. He draws on his experiences of yoga, meditation, breath, prayer, and Spirit to shed some light on the spiritual journey into God-consciousness. Additionally, some of the practices in this book are based on ancient languages including Sanskrit, Arabic and Aramaic. Last, the approach to this work is outside of conventional religious monocentrism. Rather, it is based on love, Bhakti yoga (devotional union), and mystical possibility.

OF VITAL IMPORT: "Now there are various kinds of gifts, but the same Spirit. There are various kinds of service, and the same Lord. There are various kinds of workings, but the same God, who works all things in all. But to each one is given the manifestation of the Spirit for the profit of all. For to one is given through the Spirit the word of wisdom, and to another the word of knowledge, according to the same Spirit; to another faith, by the same Spirit; and to another gifts of healing, by the same Spirit; and to another workings of miracles; and to another prophecy; and to another discerning of spirits; to another different kinds of languages; and to another the interpretation of languages. But the one and the same Spirit produces all of these, distributing to each one separately as he desires." ~ *1 Corinthians 12:4-11, World English Bible.*

CONTENTS

PREFACE

This book came about from a mystical experience I had many years ago. I awoke one morning and found myself floating out of my body, rising up through the ceiling, above the city and into the cosmos. As my consciousness observed the stars, another consciousness came within my awareness. I sensed it was benevolent so I thought,

What is your name?

"Maharishi…"

Okay so tell me Maharishi, what more is there to life than working, earning money, buying the cars, buying the homes, struggling and searching for happiness?

"Come with me."

His light-body took my hand and together we flew at high-speed down to earth and then across a desert with rolling sand dunes. Suddenly we shot down into a sand dune and came into a long underground corridor a hundred yards or more long with three-stories of jail cells lining the right and left walls with disincarnated souls wailing and flailing their arms through the jail bars. He either used his hand or a wand of some type to break open the lock of each cell, sparks flying through us each time, releasing all the souls to liberation. Upon reaching the end of the corridor we suddenly flew up through the sand into the sky and back into the cosmos.

My consciousness was speechless and awestruck.

"That's what it's about," he said, "ending human suffering."

Suddenly I woke up back in my body in my bedroom.

Ending human suffering? Ending human suffering? What did he mean, ending human suffering? Helping to free prisoners? Working in the prison ministry? Ending human suffering of false imprisonment?

This perplexed me for a couple of days and then it dawned on me. Ending human suffering of the illusion that we are separate from God!

So I entered upon the quest from that day forward to know God, commune with God, and realize who and what Spirit is.

This is what I discovered.

PROLOGUE

"Soul journey through time. Everlasting love is yours to have.
The winds of the ocean never cease refreshing the wings of
your soul. Through the breath of life you soar as the eagle,
through the wonder of sound you sing as the nightingale,
through the power of touch you feel the pleasure of baby skin.
Soul, your journey has taken you to the earth plane. You have
a life to live, it is yours, and you chart its course. You may
cherish it, you may waste it, but you have chosen to live it.
Learn, grow, and develop your character through love, virtue,
wisdom and service. And always remember, you are not alone.
If you need help, simply ask and help will be forthcoming."

INTRODUCTION

The Immortal Breath of Christ is a beacon of spiritual light in the darkness of the night on the endless flight of the soul. It's about knowledge written in the heavens for the advancement of mankind. It's about drawing on the energy patterns and knowledge of the advanced soul to accelerate your soul development and the development of the Over-Soul. It is very subtle. Attuning and resonating to the higher vibration of the Master as a path to resonating to the higher vibration of the Creator. It's about moving beyond the illusion of separation; separation from others, separation from God. Letting go of the physical world temporarily and discovering your true Self. Identifying with God, the Creative Vibration until you realize you are that, the I AM THAT I AM. Knowing and becoming the known as the knower. The knower, known, and knowing is You, not your body or mind. It is You.

Why tread this path? Liberation from suffering. Freedom from mass manipulation, mind control and the propaganda you are spoon fed each day from society. Consider the possibility that this existence you call reality is just the proverbial "tip of the iceberg." There is a higher existence right here, right now where you break free from the bonds of struggle, break free from the projected reality, and awaken to the highest path of existence your soul knows. It's time to awaken to enlightened consciousness of unconditional love, grace, beauty and truth; claim your inheritance of divine goodness; and bless others as you are blessed.

There are many way-showers of wisdom. Many paths. You have free will so pick one path, study it, walk it and see how it serves you. Stay with it for a number of weeks, months or years and see how your life changes. Walk in their footsteps until you discover your own. Some follow or walk a path of asceticism and self-denial, entering into extreme suffering as a way to God consciousness. Others take the mystic path of discipline, concentration, inner knowledge, and contemplation; whereas others practice devotion, love and service as a means to liberation. Choose the one you resonate with and walk it with all your heart. You may find it serves you or it may not, if not, choose another. What works for one may not necessarily work for another. However, the way-showers have provided you clues, both apparent and very subtle for you to understand. Some are very powerful and some are very gentle. It is your quest, your dharma, your duty to discern what those clues are and the secrets you and you alone must discover. Now is the time to journey into your consciousness, and then beyond into the consciousness of the way-showers. But don't stop there. Continue on into the consciousness of God. For you will discover, if you haven't already, that this journey you are on is infinite. It is a journey of your soul where no limits exist, where greater glory is awaiting you, and where pure love reigns. Simply remember there is no destination, only degrees of liberation. How free do you want to be?

Today is an illusion. Tomorrow is a dream. Yesterday is history. Now is the moment of what you call reality. What you have is nothing but what you are is everything. This may sound like a paradox, but it is not.

Open your mind to the possibility of words that carry a sacred resonance, meaning, and vibration as to effect healing on a very deep and profound level. What you are to do is ingest these words so that your body and mind can more fully and consciously shine the divine light into the world.

Let yourself be love. Persevere. O' Mother of all life, come forth Thou, bring Thy knowledge of freedom. Star of light, star of love, burning bright, emanation of being, an illusion of destiny, infinite, a portal to a higher world, a window to the star of God.

Lord, take me to myself so to know myself, so to love myself, so to experience love, so to love others, so to serve others, so to help others, so to remember who I am, to be and know I am. My beloved Lord, you are the window to my soul. Thy gatekeeper, lead me through the gate.

"Shh…
Woe begone my forlorn child
Lay your weary head to rest,
Forgive the soul of karmic darkness
Lest you fail to pass the test.

This life you live is one of many
Its valued state is limitless,
You came to be for single purpose
To journey on a noble quest.

The prize you seek not fame nor fortune
is one we share among all men,
It's one the senses cannot fathom
It's only known from deep within.

You've lost your way but now it's time
to light the path for you to see,
Tarry no more in dark confusion
Behold the sun, the inner-key.

Return beloved from sin of ignorance
a faultless state all men must bear,

Now climb the rungs to liberation
Keep climbing once you think you're there.

For wisdom is a noble virtue
And faith is needed in this race,
But selfless love is lord supreme
If one's to live in state of grace.

So walk the path to source of being
Sit still, be quiet and go within,
And when you see the sun arising
Soul surrender, infinuum."

Yes, thank you for your guidance my beloved Lord. I beseech you tell me more, come to me, speak to me, be of me…

"I AM is a catalyst to the mind of remembrance. Ingest the bread of life for it can be had in many ways; through breath, through word, through nature, through vision, and through the inner voice of silence. Be aware of who you are. Be aware of where you walk. What is the ground of existence upon which you place your feet? Does She not nurture you? Let the mud of Mother Earth wrap your body with its love. Let the sun of the Father dry your outer skin drawing out the poisons. Let the rain of a warm summer shower wash clean the dredge revealing your soft supple skin of innocence."

"Gently, gently, gently, one comes into an understanding of their rightful place in this world. It is a love story between you and yourself. Be kind to yourself, accept yourself, love yourself with the omnipotent love of God. The hummingbird loves the flower, and serves as God's messenger of beauty spreading His pollen of life to all of the flowers of the field. Singing, vibrating at enormous speed, transmigrating across the oceans of existence, no matter how far, how high, how deep, it lives and experiences its nature. You shall do likewise. Every word is a prayer on the lips of the beloved. So when you speak, intone your words with feeling, give that which you wish to receive, be that which you wish to become, remember that which you know, for the things you desire, you already have. Sit, be, enjoy."

"Receive, receive O' Great one. Receive that which is yours. The angels are speaking to you. Listen. Stripped away of your falseness, stand mighty and tall among the legions, knowing action to take when most powerful. Wait, wait, wait. The proper time is almost here. Reside in the silent roar of splendor. A gathering like no other. As these pages turn, each successive page shines forth the energy, more powerful than before. These words of light are shining, filling and feeding through the windows" of the soul. One finds mercy in these pages of light. One finds strength. One finds courage. The clear vibratory frequency that you can accept comes through and out this portal into your being. Accept it's healing. Charged words filled with lightning. Inside a lightning bolt. Embrace the lightning.
"Does thou claim to be a mystic?"

No, I claim to be nothing, and everything.

"Does thou wish to have a house in the woods?"

The earth is my house and I am comfortable where I find myself. I am open to receiving that which Spirit deems appropriate. Spirit, bring forth into manifestation that which I need, that which I can help others with, that which others need.

"Awaken, awaken o' angel of mercy. Spread your wings and travel to the ones whose souls call you. Talk with them on a soul level. For the wisdom of the ages transmits through each."

Revelations from the spiritual realms invites one's mind to question, 'from whence cometh forth?' The intellect likes order, science, and proof and tends to discount, disregard, or even discredit communication from Spirit. Don't short-change yourself. Spirit has much to teach and your soul has much to learn.

Now most recognize and accept the threefold distinction of our humanness: body, soul, and spirit; however sometimes there is confusion as to the difference between spirit and soul. So let's consider each aspect of our being in greater detail now.

SPIRIT

Spirit is the manifestation of God, the light, the pure clear light. Spirit always was and always will be. It pervades everything in the universe and is that which gives life, for Spirit is life. Spirit is omniscience (all knowing, intelligence beyond intelligence as we know it), omnipresence (everywhere, here and simultaneously beyond space and time), and omnipotence (inherently all powerful). Spirit is God.

The word 'spirit' translates from the Latin word *spiritus*, which means 'of the breath of life,' pertaining to, affecting or concerning the spirit or higher moral qualities, especially as regarded in a religious aspect. *Spiritus sanctus* means 'the Divine Spirit,' and *spirital* means 'pure.' All of these words are pointing the way to the realization of our true nature, for to know Spirit is to know God.

It is said that Edgar Cayce, known as the *sleeping prophet*, had the ability to enter into trance during sleep and then into God Consciousness to help heal thousands of people. Cayce has been quoted as saying, "Spirit self has been, and always will be 'before the throne of God.' This spark of God, this spirit is perfect, unblemished and made in the image of Elohim as recorded in Genesis 1:26… For ye are a corpuscle in the body of God; thus a co-creator with Him, in what ye think, in what ye do." ~ Edgar Cayce reading 2794-3

Think of it this way, a hologram of say an apple, is a projected image of millions of points of light. If you were to zoom in on each point of light you would observe the complete image of the apple. You are one of those points of light as an image of God and can awaken your consciousness to this truth by raising your spiritual consciousness through this portal. Awakening is the first step to realizing Heaven on earth, the 'abundant life' the great master teacher Jesus spoke of.

So take time to go apart into the desert of your consciousness as Jesus taught his disciples. Take time to meditate, for the healing you seek occurs in deep meditation. The wisdom you seek reveals itself, and the illusion of whatever you're struggling with dissolves in the light of truth. For instance, recently during meditation I heard,

"You are a divine child of God, you are already healed, your mind is a container of childhood memories that you believe to be You, that you believe to be the real you, but it is only an illusion. You are me and I am you, I am God, I am the Father. You can have anything you want, even wholeness, you simply have to ask. Ask and it shall be given to you, seek and you shall find. Shed the falseness and be free. Listen to God on the wind. The sense of separation is because you identify with the body. Identify with Spirit, your true Self and know God. Then the falseness of separation falls away and you realize you never left, you never lost."

Thus, now is the time to break the chains of ignorance, imprisonment, sorrow of this earthly life and come into the 'abundant life' of Spirit, love, joy and bliss that knows no bounds. For it is a heavenly love, the sweet ambrosia nectar of the gods, the elixir of life, the immortal consciousness of the Soul.

SOUL

"O' weary traveler. Drink from the well of silence. Your time is now to decide what it is you truly want in life. Be it ships to sail and lands to roam. Be it a love letter from God. You are the most magnificent birth. I adore you in all your splendor, glory and being. Walk with faith. I put you on this earth to do something for me. Read on and you will uncover the signposts that will reveal your path and destiny. Beyond time you were conceived, each aspect conceived in love. Do you not know how truly magnificent you are? Let me open your eyes. Your soul is my soul and my soul is eternal."

What is soul?

"Soul is consciousness. A learning vehicle of God that evolves, has a sense of itself yet resides in the All. It is not a particle of the universe, it has no form. It is not measured or judged."

It is not judged?

"No. The soul is experience memoried and memory experienced. Evolution, involution."

Why do we have a soul?

"It's an Oversoul aspect. All are one. One is all. Lift, lift your vibrations. Allow the soul its wings within your conscious mind. Love the soul. Listen to it."

"Who am I?
I am nothing.
Oh what a joy as nothing.
No labels, no preconceptions, no thing.

Nothingness fills everything.
It is the space between the atoms.
Nothing is pure potential,
But once actuated,
becomes something,
which has limits.

Realize nothingness and you can be anything you want.
But at that point you don't want anything,
because there is nothing to want.

Most don't understand nothing,
Because their minds are too full.
Empty one's mind to nothingness and return to Infinity.
Who am I?
I am nothing.
Oh what a joy!"

These poems come from the soul into consciousness and then through the mind. But as you see, it is so subtle like a slight breeze fleeting by on a warm summer day that stillness of the mind is necessary to notice the soul.

Some say the soul encompasses at least three subtle vehicles; the *energy body*, the *dream body*, and the *light body*. For instance:

24

The *energy body* has been called the etheric-twin or double of the physical body. According to Wikipedia, "The etheric body, ether-body, or æther body, a name given by neo-Theosophy to a vital body or subtle body propounded in esoteric philosophies is the first or lowest layer in the human energy field or aura. It is said to be in immediate contact with the physical body, to sustain it and connect it with higher bodies." Powerful healers and holy persons have the ability to project one or more energy bodies giving them the ability to appear and communicate with others in more than one place at the same time (check out the documented bilocations of; Padre Pio in *Padre Pio: The True Story* by Bernard Ruffin, Swami Pranabananda in *Autobiography of a Yogi* by Paramahansa Yogananda, and other spiritual masters: https://aleteia.org/2018/06/28/5-saints-who-could-bilocate/).

Robert Moss in his book *DreamGates* observes, "The astral body or *dream body* is a vehicle to clairvoyant sight not unlike the physical body, surrounded by an aura of flashing colors, composed of an order of fineness higher than that of physical matter, in which feelings, passions, desires, and emotions are expressed and which act as a bridge between the physical brain and the mind, the latter operating in the still higher vehicle—the mind-body.

And the *light body* is as fire or lightning, a point or curl of light. "The Gnostics called this the 'garment of light'. The Neoplatonists called it the augoeides, or 'light-formed' body. Additionally, they distinguished a 'spirit body' (pneuma) associated with the breath, and a 'celestial body,' often described as either the light-formed body (augoeides) or starry body (astroeides). And of course the Christian mystics spoke frequently of the soul. Hildegard de Bingen saw the soul taking possession of the fetus inside the womb, descending into flesh 'like a fiery globe.' She saw how soul energy travels with the breath. John of the Cross spoke of 'the garment of the soul in three colors.' And Jakob

Bohme wrote about 'subtle flesh' and a 'force-body' so subtle it could pass through stones."

John White reflects on the *light-body* in his article titled, *From Morality to Mysticism.* "In the Judeo-Christian tradition, the light-body is called 'the resurrection body' as well as 'the glorified body.' The prophet Isaiah said, 'The dead shall live, their bodies shall rise.' (~ Isaiah 26:19). St. Paul called it 'the celestial body' as well as 'the spiritual body' (soma pneumatikon). In Sufism it is called 'the most sacred body' as well as 'the supracelestial body.' In Taoism, 'the diamond body' and those who obtain it consciously are called 'the immortals' or 'the cloudwalkers.' In Tibetan Buddhism, 'the light body.' In Tantrism and some schools of yoga, 'the vajra body, the adamantine body, or the divine body.' In Kriya yoga, 'the body of bliss.' In Vedanta, 'the superconductive body.' In Gnosticism and Neoplatonism, 'the garment of light or the radiant body.' In the alchemical tradition, the Emerald Tablet calls it 'the Glory of the Whole Universe' and 'the golden body.' The alchemist Paracelsus called it 'the astral body.' In the Hermetic Corpus, it is called 'the immortal body' (soma athanaton). Some mystery schools call it 'the solar body.' In Rosicrucianism, it is called 'the diamond body of the temple of God.' In ancient Egypt, 'the luminous body or being' (akh). In Old Persia, 'the indwelling divine potential.' In Mithraic liturgy, 'the perfect body.'"

Thus, many have found through spiritual practice, devotion and will, one can consciously enter into these subtle vehicles (energy, dream, and light bodies) for the purpose of helping others, knowledge/wisdom attainment, soul development, and conscious awareness of your God-self.

For example, the following is an experience I had recently communing with my soul through what I believe to be my "dream body and higher state called the mind-body" (according to Moss' definition).

26

Soul speak to me.

"There is no place to go, nothing to do, simply be and listen. Thou art walking as a child and it can seem shaky at first, but simply let me guide you. I will always protect you for I am within you and around you."

Are you a separate being or consciousness?

"No, I come through the mind, the individual mind and the God Mind."

What is it I need to learn and share with others?

"Anyone can contact the soul. The more you reach, the closer you get to your awakened consciousness. I am here to help you during your physical incarnation, help your physical body experience health, comfort, joy, bliss, and help other souls for all are one. Come forth into the heavenly realms dear one and remember your inheritance. Remember the journey you are traveling on for it started a very long time ago. Let us journey back into the memory of consciousness known as your soul, the memory bank that stores every single occurrence in the life of the soul. Go back to the beginning. Eons and eons back further and further."

Travel at the speed of thought, at the speed of consciousness until you arrive at the bosom of the creator, the moment of conception from the mind of God. Joyous, gleeful dancing soul with billions of other dancing souls lovingly birthed into being.

"It is charted, it is written, your evolution is certain, your path is endless, your will is His will. Helpers, guides, cherubim, angelic beings have been assigned to help you on your journey. 'For He shall give His angels charge over thee, to keep thee in all thy ways.' (~ *Psalm 91:11*). Ambassadors of God, pure intention, pure protection. Listen for their guidance. Travel, gain knowledge in the schools of existence on all the realms. Advancement in the lower realms leads to the higher ones. Awareness of one realm opens possibility of awareness of the next. Are you aware? Go into the physical. Command the physical and the metaphysical will come into your greater knowledge of awareness. There is a balance. Discipline disciple. Chart your course in the physical and use the metaphysical to sail. Put the winds of Spirit into the sails of your vehicle."

Okay. Speak to me God. Really speak to me on a deep level.

"Oh little one, you are so impatient. Can you understand the meaning of quorum? The gathering of specific power of essence to put in motion the forces of nature?"

Universal nature, universal laws?

"Let life unfold for you. Don't be anxious. Be in the present like now. See your presence in everything. Manifestation is your creative realization!"

GOD CONSCIOUSNESS

"Love God more than you love yourself, although you are God, they are the ideals of God you are loving and embodying. What are your ideals? What are God's ideals? When you know God's ideals you are perfected. Strive to know, pray to know, study to know, meditate to know, walk to know, reflect to know, practice to know. Reach your hand up and I will take it and pull you up to the next level of learning, for there are many levels, many mansions. This lifetime you will make great progress. Stay in the blue pearl as you love others. The blue pearl."[1]

"Dear soul, it's about my energy. Reach with all of your essence to tap into my energy. Attune, attune, attune, like a piano wire, resonate with my love until you become my love. Then I will truly walk as you and you as I."

Are you the Christ?

"Yes, I am the Christ."

Thank you. I am sorry I doubted.

"Your mind and your ego, an aspect of your mind, cause this illusion you call doubt. When this happens, tell it you recognize it, you love your mind and ego, but you live in truth of the I AM. You will only

---

1 *The 'blue pearl' is the pineal gland, which most of all mystical traditions recognize as a portal into the spiritual realms.*

use the mind and ego for the highest good which will more than satisfy them. Stand strong, stand firm. Feel the star of the I AM inside of you."

Christ is the English word for *Christos,* a transliteration of the New Testament Greek word (some say means "*the Incarnated*") and the Old Testament Hebrew translation is *Maschiach or Messiah* meaning the *Anointed One.* God consciousness, the Universal Cosmic Consciousness incarnates as "the Christ" within. Thus, *the Christ* is the perpetual and eternal realization of the immortal God-Self, the perfected state of consciousness that Jesus of Nazareth was, is and will always be. And this is the perfected state of consciousness that each soul is progressively remembering.

Does one need to be a mystic in order to attain this Christ-centered universal consciousness? No, some come into this realization early on in life through the sheer grace of God. But for most of us, it takes spiritual discipline to reach Self-realization. That I believe is the reason for practicing mystical and spiritual practices: to train the body and mind to reach a state where the divine birth can happen. Karlfreid Durckheim, author of *The Way of Transformation* supports this when she wrote, "The real meaning of human existence is to make manifest in the world the Divine Being embodied within us, thus the true significance and bodily training lies in the need to reach a state that makes such manifestation possible."

And Norman Paulsen, practitioner of Kriya Yoga and author of *The Christ Consciousness* also supports this truth when he wrote, "The Savior of humanity is Christ Consciousness, the Christ, which destroys selfishness in the individual spirit, as well as sin, shame, guilt, and fear." He defines Christ Consciousness (also referred to as Cosmic Consciousness) as a state of consciousness that includes and transcends simple consciousness and self-consciousness. Paulsen refers to the 19th century author, Dr. Maurice Bucke, author of Cosmic

Consciousness by quoting, "Simple consciousness is feeling separate from all forms of life and focused on the instinctual needs of survival and procreation. Self-consciousness is the expression of selfishness, the desire to possess and store mental images (arts, sciences, religions), and being separate from all creation. Christ or Cosmic Consciousness includes (but is not limited to) full understanding of all life forms and images now available, intellectual and cosmic illumination, awareness of moral exaltation or sense of contribution to the human race, the soul's sense of immortality or consciousness of eternal life, and absolute knowledge from the well of eternal experiences."

THE COSMIC SENSE

Dr. Bucke, in his book *Cosmic Consciousness: A Study in the Evolution of the Human Mind*, studied and wrote about 50 people whom he suspected all experienced Cosmic Consciousness to a greater or lesser degree at some point during their life. This list includes such luminaries as Moses, Isaiah, Jesus the Christ, St. Paul, Gautama the Buddha, Plotinus, Socrates, Mohammed, Dante, Swedenborg, John Yepes *(St. John of the Cross),* Francis Bacon, William Blake, Walt Whitman, Ralph Waldo Emerson, Blaise Pascal, Ramakrishna Paramahansa, and others. Bucke identified the benchmarks of the "Cosmic Sense" as:

Subjective Light

St. John of the Cross talked about this subjective light when he wrote, "At times, the divine light strikes the soul with such force that the darkness is unfelt and the light unheeded; the soul seems unconscious of all it knows, and is therefore lost, as it were, in forgetfulness, knowing not what has happened to it, unaware of the lapse of time. It may and does occur that many hours pass while it is in this state of forgetfulness; all seems but a moment when it again returns to itself." Dr. Bucke describes it as, "suddenly, without warning, having a sense of being immersed in a flame, or rose-colored cloud, or perhaps rather a sense that the mind is itself filled with such a cloud of haze."

31

Moral Elevation

We see this observed and expressed in the Christian teachings of Jesus, the Hebrew teachings of the 10 Commandments, the Gifts of the Holy Spirit, the Fruits of the Holy Spirit, the first two limbs (yamas and niyamas) of the Eight Limbs of Yoga by Pantanjali, the Noble Eightfold Path of Buddhism, and other spiritual teachings.

Intellectual Illumination

Bucke and those he wrote about described this as "a knowingness of universal laws, a clear conception or vision of the meaning of the universe, life, relative death, and conception of the whole."

Sense of Immortality

This is clearly indicated in the teachings of Jesus, Paramahansa Yogananda, Ramakrishna, Adida Samraj, Nisagaradatta Maharaj, Bhagavan Sri Ramana Maharshi, Adi Shankara, Sri Aurobindo, Jiddu Krishnamurti, Anandamayi Ma and others.

Loss of the Fear of Death

When one realizes cosmic consciousness, death "loses its sting" *(~ 1 Corinthians 15:55)*. Sure, there is relative death, death of the physical body—that which is born must die, but that which is immortal, consciousness itself, never dies. Adida Samraj, author of *Easy Death*, and one who I believe realized Cosmic Consciousness, used to say, "No matter what arises or does not arise, there is only consciousness itself…" meaning Cosmic Consciousness.

Loss of the Sense of Sin

The illusion of sin, that which to feel guilty of, evaporates in the light of Cosmic Consciousness.

Suddenness of the Awakening

Bucke describes it as, "Like a dazzling flash of lightning in a dark night, revealing that which had been hidden in clear view." It's as if suddenly one's awareness has direct knowledge and viewpoint of omniscience and omnipresence.

Previous Character of the Individual

"Refers to the individual already possessing a relatively good physique, good health and above all else, an exalted moral nature, strong sympathies, warm heart, courage, and a strong and earnest religious feeling," he said. There are always exceptions to this, citing the life of Saul, persecutor of Christians until he was suddenly enlightened and then known as Paul.

Age of Illumination

Bucke points out the majority of what he believed to be cases of Cosmic Consciousness occurred between the age of 35 to 45 years old. However, he noted there were some younger and some older.

Added Charm to the Personality so that Others are Strongly Attracted to that Person

"Many who appear to have or have had attained Cosmic or Christ Consciousness became teachers, writers, poets, etc. and there seems to be a divine purpose and reason for this added charm," Bucke reasoned, "I suspect to help humanity evolve spiritually."

Transfiguration of the Subject, as Seen by Others, When the Cosmic Sense is Actually Present

Dante said he "was transhumanized *or transfigured* into a God."

Many way-showers have attempted to shed light on the inner-journey to God. St. Teresa of Avila talks of the seven chambers or levels of spiritual development in the *Interior Castle*. She also gave us *The Way of Perfection.* John Yepes (St. John of the Cross) wrote of the inner-journey in his *Dark Night of the Soul,* as well as *The Spiritual Canticle of the Soul and The Bridegroom Christ.* St. Ignatius of Loyola brought forth his *Spiritual Exercises.* Patanjali brought forth the *Yoga Sutras.* Julian of Norwich gave us *Revelations of Divine Love.* And one of my favorites, *The Cloud of Unknowing,* is an anonymous fourteenth-century text consisting of a series of letters written by a monk to his disciple in the way of Divine union. It sheds light and methodology of which to experience the subjective light and ultimately awaken to God consciousness.

Guidance from these spiritual pilgrims (and others) through their writings, attunement to their energy, alignment with their philosophy, and practice of their techniques are all 'stepping-stones' across the river Styx (where the gods swore their most solemn oaths).

So sail across the stormy waters of doubt, blaze the trail through the forest of despair, cross the desert of winds until you finally reach the mountain of liberation and then climb. Climb, climb, climb on the instructions of the Masters. And always remember, "Ask and it shall be given you, seek and you shall find, knock and it shall be opened unto you." ~ *Matthew 7:7*

COMMUNING WITH
THE DIVINE

God is deep in the forest. The coolness of the forest is joyful in the heat of the day. Allow me to lead Thou to the sacred place. The sacred place where the soul dwells. Keep following the path now deeper and deeper into the forest. Take your time, there is no hurry. Smell the humus of the earth, the greenery of the ferns and pines. Now you are under the canopy of the forest; streams of light, rays of sun are streaming through the tree canopy. This is a magical place as you stop, stand on the path, and look into the magic. The magic of God's beauty and love. As you gaze across the forest floor, you notice a pattern in the way the rays of light are shining through the trees. They are illuminating an invisible path, which is becoming more and more visible in your heightened sense of awareness. You leave the path you are on and start for this path of light, knowing full well you will return to your life path when ready. You slowly walk this path of light deeper and deeper into the forest. You are being led by God. This light path is showing you the way. You walk carefully, slowly and methodically, placing one foot in front of the other as you continue to step along this path of light. It is winding its way like a snake into the forest, deeper and deeper. The trees are getting thicker and thicker until it is almost like a maze labyrinth of light. You have no fear, for "Thou art with me." The Twenty-third Psalm flashes through your mind. You walk on. You turn a bend and come out into a clearing within the forest. It is twenty five to fifty feet in diameter, open sky, sunlight shining down illuminating it brightly, soft moss covered ground you step upon, like a bed of green velvet, you walk out into the center of this sacred place. As you approach the middle of this clearing, bathed in God's glorious light, you notice a small gold box, laying on a flat stone, a snow-white stone like a piece of alabaster, but perfectly flat and shiny. This small box is made of gold, it is shaped like a book, it looks like a book, ornately fashioned with exquisite designs on the front, binding, and back. You stoop down and slowly touch the gold box running your fingers over the emblazoned design, a heavenly design, a mystical design. *Fleur de lis*, scrollwork, crescent moon on the cover at the bottom, a sacred fish in the center, a golden disk above, cherubim in the corners, and Aramaic writing inscribed on the cover and binding. You pick up the box now. It is heavy, very heavy for such a small gold box, approximately four by seven inches and two and a half inches deep. Does it open? Yes, it is hinged so you open the gold box. As you do the blinding light of God shines forth from within filling you and all of the forest with bright light. You still feel the gold box in your hands but cannot see it. Placing your hand in the box you feel a cover, a book filling the entire inside of the box. You remove the book from the gold box. It is white. Gold edge pages, leather bound, white leather. Gold lettering on its front. This is the book you have longed for. It is the key you've been seeking. It is yours to ingest, the secrets of humanity's soul, the healing words of God, the spiritual catalyst of remembrance. Suddenly you notice it has become bread, freshly baked bread still hot from the hearth. The deep aroma wafts through your senses returning memories of earlier times when you were safe and loved. You can't resist and begin to tear off pieces and eat it. It is simply scrumptious, the more you eat, the more you are in heaven. It is indescribably delicious. You have eaten half. With each bite, it tastes even more heavenly than before. You finish the book, licking all the buttery sweetness and goodness from your fingers. Looking down, you see the open gold box on the white stone. What can you leave in the gold box? You leave your tears, the tears of disappointments you have suffered in your life, the tears of illusioned abandonment, the illusory

36

abandonment your mind and emotions have projected, the tears of guilt, shame and regret of mistakes long past. Yes, you weep, filling the box with your tears, cleansing your humanness. After you have wept purging yourself until there is no more at this time to shed, you close the cover of the box. Now you stand in this beautiful sacred space, outstretch your arms to the heavens, look up and surrender to God.

Indwelling Spirit, I am yours, O' guide me along your paths of righteousness, lift me with your love and strength, enlighten my mind so that I may be your instrument of love, peace and hope. I am ready and willing to hear your guidance. I decree, "ALMA NAHRA AUMEN-EL, AHA" three times louder and louder each time emanating from the depths of my soul.

"Shh… become the path upon which you tread, for the path has already arrived. The path sustains you, transfigures you, and leads you back to me."

Communing with the Divine is your birthright. One way to do this is through your *Ishta Devata* (Sanskrit for *one's personal form of the Divine*). Your Ishta Devata is a personification of a Deity that you feel very close to (or would like to) that embodies the characteristics you would like to have. Depending on your religious upbringing, one's Ishta may be Jesus, Mother Mary, Kwan Yin, Shiva, Ganesha, Krishna, Babaji, Mohammed, Buddha, one of the Saints, etc. The main reason to commune (converse, talk over, share time) with your Ishta is to open your heart to experience oneness, your God-nature.

When I was studying to become a certified meditation instructor a number of years ago, we were instructed to select a personal form of the Divine of which to establish communion with. During that time, I found myself drawn to Kwan Yin, Goddess of Compassion, a form of the Divine Feminine Whenever I gazed upon her image, my heart opened up and feelings of love, compassion, and benevolence flooded my body and consciousness. I simply knew that she was the form of the Divine for my devotional practice.

When I first started to commune with Kwan Yin, I found it awkward. My mind kept saying I was unworthy. *Who am I to think this Goddess would help me when others deserve her presence and help more?* But as I persevered I began to enter into relationship with her. She revealed many deep lessons to me during my meditations. Lessons in how to allow more compassion to flow through me, how to give selfless service to others, how to see the beauty in others, myself, nature and the universe. Like a close friend, Kwan Yin has been there for me whenever I've needed her.

For instance, one morning, after many months of communing with her, I had a problem and needed her specific help. I was having trouble trying to quiet my mind during meditation. I prayed to her for help. She said,

"Hold an image of me sitting in meditation, within your mind's eye *(known as the third eye, brow chakra or sun center).* Now looking closely at my image and within my sun center seeing an image of you sitting in meditation. Zooming in on that image of you, looking closely at its sun center and seeing an image of me sitting in meditation. Zooming in on that image of me, looking closely at its sun center and seeing an image of you sitting in meditation...." As I followed her instructions, going deeper and deeper into the images, I lost all track of thinking. Before I knew it, I was in a deep state of meditation. I experienced my universal nature and believe me, no words can describe it. It's beyond anything one can imagine.

Interestingly enough, after nine months of communing with Kwan Yin, another form of the Divine began to show up in my life, both as external images and as an internal yearning. After much contemplation, I decided it was time to change my Ishta. I kept telling myself that I would do the ritual I was taught, but I kept putting it off. You see, I had a close relationship with Kwan Yin, had learned many things from her, and simply did not want to bid her farewell. I have had many conversations with her, walked with her in her temple and gardens, watched her feed the animals, and have asked for and received guidance from her. But one weekend, I had a mystical experience directly relating to my need to bid her farewell from my daily communion.

It was a windy Saturday, overcast and raining on and off. We have a pond in our backyard with a few goldfish and koi in it, and I decided to step outside and look at the fish. I noticed a piece of paper had blown into the pond and was sitting on the bottom. With slight irritation I was thinking, *"Oh great, a piece of garbage in my pond."* Well, the weather was mucky, the wind was kicking up, so I went inside with the intention of retrieving that paper later. The next day was a beautiful sunny Sunday. I was out back enjoying the sun and nature, and noticed the paper in the pond. So I went around to the other side of the pond, stepped out on the furthest rock, stooped down and reached deep into the water. It was on the bottom and I could barely reach it, but finally was able to snag it with my fingers. As I stood up, preparing to wad it up, I noticed it was a piece of sheet music and since I play the piano, I decided to dry it out and see what it sounded like. So I laid it on the picnic table in the sun to dry. A few hours later I was walking by the table and noticed it. This is what it says:

> "I call to Thee for Thou wilt answer me. I call to Thee, Lord,
>   I call.
> To Thee, O Lord, King of all. I call to Thee, Lord most holy.
>   Thee, Lord most holy.
> I call to Thee who wilt answer me. To Thee I call, Lord, King
>   of all.
> I call to Thee, Lord most holy. Thee, Lord most holy.

I call to Thee who wilt answer me. To Thee I call, Lord, King
of all.
I call to Thee, Lord most holy. Thee, Lord most holy."

This message talked directly to me. This message that flew from the
sky into my pond for me to find was my prompting to begin my daily
communion with Jesus.

THE PORTAL

"Come with me," he said. I take his hand and step into the portal. We glide effortlessly into the light. What am I thinking? I close my eyes. Being led by Jesus across the fathoms of sky. God's country. Ethereal mountains. *Take me to the Father.* He is taking me to the Father. Faster and faster. Accelerating our vibrations. Buzzing sound. Deafening roar. Pervades everything. Swallowed up in a whirlwind, the center of the whirlwind, the cyclone. Silence. No vision, only absence of sound, absence of thought. Waiting. Still holding my hand.

"What do you want? What do you want soul?"

Wholeness.

"So be it. You shall have it."

Streams of light from without turning on all around me pointing into my being, pinpointing, culminating their beams into my core at my solar plexus. More and more, all around me, the point of essence is shining brighter and brighter filling me with God's light, my inner-light is gaining strength and power filling my entire being. Instantaneously it reverses, my inner light shining out in all directions from my heart shining brightly, slowly revolving, beaming my beacon out beyond for millions and millions of miles. Light person. Egg of light, ball of light, magnificent benevolent God light. Still holding onto his hand. He lets go of my hand as I float on my own revealing my true self, my inner light of essence, my aspect.

"Are you ready?"

For what?

"To return."

No, I would like to stay here for a little while longer. I am the sun. I am the light. Allow me to shine light from my heart outward consciously henceforth. Amen.

After (what I believe to be) a time, He takes my hand and we travel through the dimensions to the portal.

Thank you Jesus.

The next day...

"Come with me." He reaches out his hand, I take it and the Christ and I walk into the light.

"Be aware. Notice everything."

The light is blinding bright white and is getting brighter. It permeates all, no more darkness anywhere. We keep walking. Floating forward. Streams of rays, angelic beings, love, translucent, each with their own inner light, floating. They are glad to see me. Billions of them. Instant thought communication. Welcome. The aspects. They are called the Aspects. I too am an Aspect of God having an earth experience. All the Aspects are individual but unified as one whole together. Waves of vibration. The billions of Aspects are like a sea. Everywhere. Even within my ethereal form on this journey.

Where are we going Jesus?

"Too many questions, just be and observe."

Clearer and clearer pure light. Pure clear light, no longer light, but vibration, higher and higher vibrations. Up forward, every which way at once, expansive to the far reaches and beyond the universes.

"Attune to beyond. Beyond."

I'm not feeling good.

Back in the physical.

"Jeffrey?"

Yes Jesus?

"You will get used to the higher vibrations. Just relax and breathe AUM."

The Next Day While Sitting in Meditation...

"The key is realization, realization that you are already everything you need, the realization that you are all. Sit in silence now. Listen. Beyond the mountains of tomorrow rise the clouds of yesteryear. Go through the clouds, don't tarry but observe what you see and I will join you."

He vanishes from the portal. I am ready. I step into the light and move forward. Amazing speed. Brighter and brighter. Across a desert plane. Mountains in the distant. Over the mountain ranges. Into the clouds. Still the white light shining through the vapor. A fog. Breaking through the clouds, above the clouds, white light. I am the light. Clear light. Vibration faster and faster. Sympathetic vibration with God. Invisible. Omnipresence. Attune.

"Hello dear one. Just relax and be one with God. Reside in the pure clear vibrations of God. Practice going into the light and becoming the light multiple times a day until it becomes natural to be the light constantly."

The first time I saw Jesus in my inner-visionary state I will never forget. He was dressed in pure white raiment, sitting cross-legged in meditative prayer gazing into the vast abyss of God's light. He was communing with the Father. Interestingly enough, his back was to me. I realized this to be a profound blessing and teaching, pointing me the way to "go unto my Father." *~ John 14:6*

There are many portals, or windows, through which one may travel into the higher realms. The bindu (point) of light, the star you see in your 'sun center' at the top of the nose between the eyes when sitting in meditation practice is the one I travel through.

"The lamp of the body is the eye: if therefore your eye is sound, your whole body will be full of light." *~ Matthew 6:22*

AWAKENING TO SPIRIT

"In its original state, the soul was feathered all over. So now it is all in a state of ferment and throbbing; in fact the soul of a man who is beginning to grow his feathers has the same sensations of pricking and irritation and itching as children feel in their gums when they are just beginning to cut their teeth." ~ Plato, Phaedrus

What is my grand purpose?

"You know, it is written in your memory. Soul maturity. Soul evolution. Soul growth."

How can I accomplish my purpose?

"Your purpose is always being accomplished. For now, simply and consciously be aware of energy (vibration), light, and intention. These three things accelerate your growth, potentiate your growth, and nurture your growth. Energy is that which is and never dies, it just changes form, like the water in the sea that evaporates changing into airborne particles, clouds, mist, steam, rain, and ice. Be aware of subtle things, note the things that affect and effect you, what is good for you, and when you feel most energetic. Do those things that get you in touch with your energy and the energy of the infinite. There is a dance between these two, yes, you do dance. Continue to visit the Source, draw your lessons, draw from the well, practice that which you learn, that which you learn is always available, the mind is a wonderful tool but remember it is not you, it is simply a tool. Cultivate the seeds you are planting, plant and water them in fertile soil, the soil of your mind and body. The seeds of consciousness grow like the mighty oak. It is pure and majestic. Draw the energy, use the energy. It is yours to use so tap into it daily multiple times through the exercises you will find within these pages. Tap into it from nature. Tap into it from scripture. It will come to you from many sources, this Divine energy. Discern what serves you best at a particular time in your lifecycle and open your chalice and receive. The thousand-petalled lotus is not just for connection with the source. It is for... it is a portal, like there are many portals, some of which you are already being made aware of."

This portal into God Consciousness is the sacred place within that can be approached and crossed over into within the quietude of meditation, prayer, and dreams. It is the Holy Grail, the treasure beyond all earthly treasure and it is the inheritance of each soul. "It is your birthright as a Child of God to claim your inheritance—and if children, then heirs, heirs of God, and joint-heirs with Christ." ~ *Romans 8:17*. This quest for the Holy Grail holds many challenges, tests of faith, and encounters with fear and pain. Just remember God is always with you.

THE BREATH OF THE SOUL

"The spirit of God hath made me,
and the breath of the Almighty hath given me life." ~ *Job 33:4*

The breath is of great mystical significance because it is a path into infinity. Breathing is what all living entities do, from the mineral kingdom, the earth breathes, from the plant kingdom, the plants breathe, and of course from the animal kingdom, we breathe. Breath is life. Breathing in the prana of life through all pores, all molecules, the breath sustains you. One can live on the breath of God alone. There are a number of Saints who have done this for weeks, months, and even years. For instance, it's been documented that Therese Neumann, Juliana of Cornillion, Margaret of Hungary, Margaret of Cortona, Catherine of Genoa, Padre Pio of Petrilcina, and many others have lived solely on the breath of God for the latter part of their life.

Breath is the I AM. Feel your breathing. Enjoy it, for it is a gift. Breathe in the silkiness of life for it is pleasing. Rest, relax, release, breathe. Just breathe in each moment. Observe the breath pattern. Like a baby breathes abdominally, full body breathing, full of life, open to all possibilities, all potential, take flight on the breath. Higher and higher, soaring higher and higher, flapping the wings of Spirit through the breath. Breath is freely given. Lighten your heaviness of life by breathing deeply and fully. Release the past, release the sorrow, and release the burdens through the breath. On each breath in, breathe

the cleansing breath of God and on each breath out release that which you need to release. Once the breath has purified your vehicle, breathe in through your entire vehicle (your skin) and breathe out through your entire vehicle. As you breathe out, extend your breath farther and farther away from you, first a few feet out surrounding your physical body and then double it, double it again, and again, and again onto infinity. Like a vortex sucking in the energy and then reversing, flowing out. Ten, a hundred, a thousand, etc. onto infinity. Pure clear pranic energy from the universe. Like a vacuum, like a nova. On and on and on and on and on and on continuing on to infinity. Breath is shallow now resting as I continue to expand to infinity. I AM THAT I AM. I AM THAT. Aeon angel wings. Still the breath and know God. "Be still and know that I am God." ~ *Psalm 46:10*. Dichotomy of breathing and not breathing. Breathe until the breath breathes you. The breath of the soul. Now let go of the breath and be. For when you let the breath find you, it breathes you. Foster your breathing, for it is your well-being, it is life, it is joy. Are you seeking happiness? Breathe happiness. Breathing happiness in, breathing happiness out. With each breath I take I am realizing happiness. Are you seeking abundance? Breathe abundance. Breathing abundance in, breathing abundance out. With each breath I take, I am realizing abundance. Are you seeking love? Breathe love. Breathing love in, breathing love out. With each breath I take, I am realizing love. Know what you are seeking, what you want in life, and breathe it at least five minutes a day until it becomes You. Wisdom. Peace. Health. God.

Contemporary Scholar, Neal Douglas Klotz in his book, *Prayers of the Cosmos,* discusses some of the beatitudes of Jesus, "The familiar translation, 'Blessed are the poor in spirit' ~ *Matthew 5:3* in proper Aramaic-to-English translation is, 'Happy and aligned with the One are those who find their home in the breathing.'

And Rumi, famous Sufi mystic wrote, "There is one way of breathing that is shameful and constricted. Then there's another way: a breath of love that takes you all the way to infinity."

One way to infinity (God) is through the practice of Pranayama. Prana *in Sanskrit,* means life-breath, the life-force energy also known as chi, vital airs, or life-trons. It exists in everything in the world, a life-force energy in all matter. And Yama means control. Thus, Pranayamas are breathing techniques for controlling the life energy flow in and around the body. The purpose of practicing Pranayama is to cleanse the bodies (physical, astral and mental) as well as provide greater discipline and health to the physical body, increase ability to concentrate or study, and achieve higher states of consciousness.

Learning to control your breath is the first step to learning to control your mind, your autonomic functions, your blood pressure, your physiology, and your brain waves (for when you begin to do this, new levels of awareness begin to open). Try this. Close your eyes, inhale deeply, now on exhalation silently in your mind say, 'rest, relax, release, be.' On inhalation simply enjoy the bliss of filling the lungs with life-giving oxygen and pranic energy. On exhalation (and stretched across the entire exhale) silently say, 'rest, relax, release, be.' Breathe this sequence over and over again for a few minutes now, resting, relaxing and releasing into the stillness of the moment, allowing the breath to ebb and flow like the ocean.

One of the core pranayamas I've used for years is as follows. Find a place to sit where you won't be disturbed. Turn you cell phone off and eliminate any distractions. Close your eyes and begin to take some deep breaths through the nose. Now on each inhalation and throughout the entire inhalation silently count 1..2..3..4..5. With each exhalation and throughout the entire exhalation silently count 5..4..3..2..1. Repeat this pattern for four more sets. After you practice this frequently over a few days, you can lengthen the breathing by counting higher. Notice the stillness between the numbers and between the breaths. That's where the meditation is. There are some yogi's who count the breath up to 50 or higher on the in-breath and similarly on the out-breath so don't underestimate this simple but powerful method. Last, if you count up to five then breathe five sets. If you count up to seven then breathe seven sets, and so forth.

Thus, through conscious breathing and the practice of pranayama, one can absorb, store, and transmit prana to improve vitality, overcome disease, extend physical longevity, bring about serenity, experience inner-peace and ultimately realize God-consciousness.

In conclusion, listen to the breath of God, become the breath of God, breathe the breath of God. Be the breath of God, for it is the swelling of the ocean, the ebb and flow of the tide, the gentle rain soaking the earth, releasing the gases of decay, it's the eternal circle of life itself.

"And the LORD God formed man of the dust of the ground,
and breathed into his nostrils the breath of life *[AHA]*;
and man became a living soul." ~ *Genesis 2:7*

THE LIGHT OF GOD

"Dare to love the love of Heaven,
and breathe the breath of Christ,
for you're the Light,
the Light of God
come forth, be born, take flight."

Allow the Christ seed to grow within your consciousness. Allow the birth of Christ to blossom within your soul. Allow the miracle to happen. Call forth, decree it to be so, see the light dispelling the darkness, magnify the light, breathe the light, silent chant, see the light within, feel the light and love of the indwelling Christ.

I am the clear light of God. As I journey along the path of life, helpers one at a time join me on my path. They walk beside me and talk with me when I need it most. The path is always wide enough for two to walk side by side. Sometimes they come from the right, sometimes from the left. Sometimes they stay a while, other times very briefly. But they always have something to say that benefits me. Am I listening?

"Walk with me on the path of life. Learn the wisdom that is yours. For you have walked this path many times before and you have seen many wonderful things."

In the beginning when particles of substance didn't exist, everything was already in the mind of God; everything was pure potential, yet unformed. God's nature is becoming. Becoming, being, coming into creation. Infinite creation. Infinite evolution. Infinite manifestation. This creation process has been evolving ever since and each human is responsible for being a conduit for God to manifest. So the key is knowing this and allowing this to manifest in all of its glory. Why struggle? Why not just say okay? Why not just look to the heavens and say, *Let Thy will be done.* When you do this you are setting into motion powerful forces of the universe, powerful forces of the original will and purpose God deems. This gets you in touch with your birthright, to manifest God as human. You are God. Oh, some of you will say that is blasphemy, but the fact is, you are God. You are made in his image, you have free will, and you have the power to create. You create, you give birth, you dream, think, plan, design, create. Why limit yourself to three-dimensional thinking? Do you think God approves of little thinking? He loves you unconditionally, and is proud of you no matter what, but He is happy when you finally awaken from your slumber, your confusion, your sin of ignorance. How to do this you ask? Practice going beyond the body/mind complex through meditation. And what ignorance you ask? The ignorance of the ego mind. The ignorance of the sense perceptions.

Rest in the silence, still the mind, let your consciousness flow as a still river, clear, barely moving, but always evolving. Let yourself be you. Let your Self be you, for it is you. Go higher and higher until you reach the light of consciousness, until you find the inner stillness of pure clear light and then rest in the light. So pure, so clear. There is no place to go, nothing to do, just sit in the bliss. All pervading light getting brighter and brighter.

"Listen. Hear. Who must you be? Nothing. Feel your third eye pulsate. It is radiating to me. Receive that which your mind can process. The more you open it, the more I will send. Listen through your eye. Accept the wisdom flowing to you, I am charging your vehicle, open your eye further and receive that which is yours. White beautiful light flowing into your brow chakra infused with lightning bolts of small triangles. Filling your being with light. Shining star, illumined being. Angel, take flight to the schools of eternity. There you will rediscover that which you know. The more you learn, the more you remember, *soul star*. Allow the light to heal, become the white light, then the clear light. Hear the ocean. In the ocean of existence are mind forms. Other's mind forms, your mind forms. Anytime you want to change, change your consciousness by changing what is your mind form. Clear light is the most powerful concept your mind can comprehend at this time. Be clear light. Raise your vibration. Hold the clear light. Surround yourself, wrap yourself, and infuse yourself in clear light. Wrap others in clear light. Blessings my child."

"Let the tears of God cleanse the earth, the earth of your body. Let the breath of God purify your karma, colored by experience. Let the light of God reveal your soul. Bring forth the light from within allowing it to shine brighter and brighter filling every cell, every space in your being. As the sun burns brighter and brighter, so too shall your light burn away the dross of living. Feel the baptismal fire of your soul purify and cleanse you. Brighter, and brighter and brighter... like an inner star bursting into super nova. One big sun. You are the light. Now, shine forth across the galaxies of existence, growing brighter at your source, reaching farther and farther, A thousand times the size of the sun, a billion times, surrendering to infinity. Pure clear light. Everywhere."

THE PRAYER OF GOD-CONSCIOUSNESS

Lovely lady on a waterfall of flowers, the divine feminine of angels in my life, where art thou? Come forth and dance among the clouds until the clouds disappear and all that remains is truth.

"For the truth shall free you and then you shall soar into the sun and beyond from the bright light to the clear light of God. Come with me."

Okay, let us go.

Very bright, brighter and brighter, blinding light where we need no sight, where we understand all. No emotion, just memory of emotion. It is.

"Create what you will. Create with the consciousness on the causal plane of existence. What do you want to create? Don't limit yourself."

Perfect harmony of life. Perfect balance in all things. All conditions. Acceptance, knowledge, knowing the perfect order of His will. Peace everywhere. The Christ mind.

"You are the Christ mind. What are the ideals of God? Attune to the ideals of God. It's not about you; it's about soul growth and evolution. How can your soul grow and evolve? Is there anything you can do to effect this? Yes. Pray. Pray for the children of the world who have no homes. Pray for the men and women of the world who are lost. Pray for the peace that is boundless. Pray for heaven on earth to be realized. Pray and it shall manifest. Pray, believe, and rejoice, for all prayers are answered."

I AM LORD'S PRAYER[2]
by Jesus the Christ

Our Father who art in heaven,
Hallowed be thy name, I AM.
I AM thy Kingdom come
I AM thy Will being done
I AM on earth even as I AM in heaven
I AM giving this day daily bread to all
I AM forgiving all Life this day even as
I AM also all Life forgiving me
I AM leading all men away from temptation
I AM delivering all men from every evil condition
I AM the Kingdom
I AM the Power and
I AM the Glory of God in eternal, immortal manifestation –
All this I AM.

---

2 From *Maitreya on the Image of God* by Elizabeth Clare Prophet (reprinted permission)

AUM IS THE GREAT
LIFE AMULET

Coming from a yoga meditation background, I discovered chanting AUM (also spelled OM) is a way to attune to the un-manifest Holy Spirit of Creation. Additionally, there is compelling evidence including documented eyewitness accounts as written in ancient scrolls in India and Tibet that during *the lost years of Jesus*, he travelled to the East to teach and study with the ancient way-showers of wisdom (see *The Christ of India* by Abbot George Burke, *The Lost Years of Jesus* by Elizabeth Clare Prophet, and others). Thus, it is very likely he practiced chanting AUM with the enlightened masters. Consider the possibility that chanting AUM is a much-revered secret of enlightenment. Here's why: Swami Krishnananda from The Divine Life Society in India (where yoga, meditation, astrology, and ayurvedic medicine is said to have originated 4000 – 6000 + years ago) speaks about the scriptures known as the Vedas, Samhitas, Upanishads, Bhagavad Gita and others when he wrote, "The Upanishads are secret teachings containing wisdom beyond the realm of the earth and revealing proclamations of the great sages on the nature of Reality. Among the Upanishads, the Mandukya (attributed to a great sage called Manduka) may be regarded as the most important, for it is said if you are able to understand the true meaning of this Upanishad, there may not be a necessity to study any other...the Mandukya Upanishad commences with a solemn declaration, 'The Imperishable is OM, and it is 'all this'. Everything else, whatever be of the past, present or future, is like an exposition, explanation or commentary on the meaning of this great Truth,—the Imperishable Om. Everything is Om, indeed.' This is how the Upanishad begins. 'All this, whatever is visible, whatever is cognizable, whatever can come within the purview of sense-perception, inference or verbal testimony, whatever can be comprehended under the single term, creation, all this is OM.'"

Krishnananda states in his interpretation of the Mandukya Upanishad, "Matter itself is said to have proceeded from sound and OM is said to be the most sacred of all sounds. It is the sound which preceded the universe at the time of creation. The Upanishads say that OM is God in the form of sound. It is the "root" syllable (mula mantra), the cosmic vibration that holds together the atoms of the world and heavens."

Krishnanada continues, "When you recite AUM properly, you are entering into a meditative mood. You are creating a vibration that melts all other vibrations and puts an end to cravings and creates desire for the Universal. As fire burns straw, this desire for the Universal burns up all other desires. Reciting AUM even three times correctly done, is enough to burn up all sins, to put a cessation to all desire and make you calm, quiet, and satisfied within yourself."

Note: Although they represent the same concept, OM is a monosyllabic word and AUM is a tri-syllabic word. OM is pronounced the way it is written and AUM is pronounced the way it is chanted.

As I was taught, the correct way to chant AUM is: (A) starts in the back of the mouth, (U) travels in between to finally reach the lips (M). Krishnananda wrote, "The last part of the sound AUM (the M) known as ma or makar, when pronounced makes the lips close. This is like locking the door to the outside world and instead reaching deep inside our own selves, in search of the Ultimate truth."

And Paramahansa Yogananda who wrote *The Second Coming of Christ*, speaks of AUM when he states, "…the outward manifestation of the omnipotent Christ Consciousness, its *witness* (Revelation 3:14), is AUM, the Word or Holy Ghost: an invisible divine power, the only doer, the sole causative and activating force that upholds all creation through vibration… AUM the blissful Comforter is heard in meditation and reveals to the devotee the ultimate Truth, bringing "all things to… remembrance."

Breathe AUM and you will discover it is a key to realization of omnipresent, omniscient, omnipotent Christ Consciousness. For it is no surprise in the Aramaic language Jesus the Christ spoke, the word "Aumen-el" (later pronounced Emmanuel or Immanuel) is translated as "God is with us[3]."

---

3 https://mainfacts.com/aramaic-english-dictionary-words

THE ETERNAL CALM

One method of realizing the eternal calm of wisdom is through concentration. Pick one object (your Ishta Devata, a candle flame, AUM symbol, Sri Yantra or another sacred symbol to you) and give it your undivided attention for five minutes. Every time your mind wanders and you become aware it is wandering, return to your object of concentration.

Goswami Kriyananda, spiritual preceptor from the Temple of Kriya Yoga where I received my meditation training, describes concentration as "a narrowing of attention by one's own will... It is a movement of awareness from an object to objectless inwardness (from external consciousness to internal consciousness), a transition away from things to the Reality behind those things." It is one-pointedness of mind where everything else falls away, eventually revealing truth.

Thus, the best way to describe this is through experience. I was sitting practicing meditation one morning at 5:30 a.m. silently chanting AUM while concentrating (holding within my minds eye an illuminated AUM symbol). This symbol is very beautiful and made of pure light. After a time, my consciousness either began to move toward the symbol or the symbol towards me, I was not quite sure at the time and it did not matter. As the symbol got closer and closer, larger and larger, my consciousness realized it could direct where it would merge with the symbol. Selecting the bindu (which represents the unmanifest), my consciousness knew it was going to enter this point of light. At the moment of entry, I experienced oneness with the ALL, the eternal calm where meditation is. No words can describe it.

BE STILL AND KNOW
THAT I AM GOD

"You came to earth millions of years ago, eons ago. This is the playground of life, the garden of the physical, the creative substance manifested. You feel comfortable on earth, you enjoy some of the earthly pleasures but never forgetting your heavenly roots. You are that, a pleasure made manifest. No matter what you say or think or do, you will always be the life spark itself in manifestation. Rejoice in all of your splendor. Awaken brothers and sisters to the truth within you. Harmonize with the Good, God that created you, and you can have anything you want. Let go of your bindings. Ask God to help. Seek the invisible fruit that will sustain you and feed your family. Seek the clear light of love that nourishes you and sanctifies your soul. Seek the grace and blessing of Thy Father. Accept it now. O Holy One, thou art magnificent. Rest in the stillness and I will enlighten you."

BE STILL AND KNOW THAT I AM GOD[4]
BE STILL AND KNOW THAT I AM
BE STILL AND KNOW THAT
BE STILL AND KNOW
BE STILL AND
BE STILL
BE

BE STILL AND KNOW THAT I AM GOD
BE STILL AND KNOW THAT I AM
BE STILL AND KNOW THAT
BE STILL AND KNOW
BE STILL AND
BE STILL
BE

BE STILL AND KNOW THAT I AM GOD
BE STILL AND KNOW THAT I AM
BE STILL AND KNOW THAT
BE STILL AND KNOW
BE STILL AND
BE STILL
BE

---

4 Psalm 46:10

THE SUB ROSA

What judgments do I have about myself? Judgments of unworthiness.

"You are worthy. You are worthy, You are worthy. Take yourself off the hook of unworthiness. Here, what are you unworthy to eat?"

Nothing Lord, I have free will and I can eat anything, anything at all.

"Then remember, what you feed your body, mind, and soul, you become. You are one of the chosen ones, as are all my children. And because you are chosen, you have a responsibility. A responsibility to allow me to manifest through you. Is there a word or a sign or a symbol that you can use to bring me back into your presence of acceptance until it is eternally in your mind?"

Yes, there are many.

"What is it that reminds you of me, the Father, not just reminds, but you know without a shadow of a doubt that it is I?"

God, there are so many, a lightening bolt, a flower, a rainbow, a circle, the infinity sign, a sunrise, water.

"Yes, water. That is the sign you shall use. You are water, you are holy, all water, all fluid no matter what form, it is I the I AM. Drink me and I sustain you, purify you, cleanse you. Let me fall gently on your fields of consciousness and your crops of goodness will grow. Baptize others and they're renewed in my love. Know me, one drop of water, the molecules of silky substance, a substantial element, my power lies within the atoms. Can you unlock it with the key I have given you?"

"Drink from the fountain of wisdom and awaken to the heavenly light of your own soul, the soul of God. You are a role model not only for your children, but for all children. Your actions, accomplishments, decisions are being recorded in the annals of history for eternity. Are you proud of your life thus far? If yes, then I applaud you. If no, then I applaud you for awakening sooner than later. Now is the time to change. Now is the time to love unconditionally. Now is the time to move into the light of right living and right thinking and right being. What is right and what is wrong? You know deep in your soul. Will you continue to belong to the tribe? Will you continue to give up your beliefs for the beliefs of the tribe? Are your decisions based on fear or love? Do you believe in the overall good, God, of humanity or do you have a cynical view that humanity is barbaric and needs to be controlled by power and ruthlessness? Search, search within you. What do you believe? Do you not think your soul loves all other souls on a soul level? Come into the light each day consciously. Even for a few minutes each day. Slowly increase over time until you spend more time as you know it in the light of God. Your life will change for the better, more free-flow, greater harmony, greater peace. One day you will awaken that you have never left the light, that the light is you pervading all eternity. You will see it and know it and will realize you always could fly, always could love, always could serve. Practice my beloved, for this is a key, this is a secret (the sub rosa), one of many."

THE CALL OF THE ANGEL
EMISSARIES OF GOD

"The halo of light around your countenance shines as a heavenly glow. Divinity bathes you, Your divinity bathes you, washes away dirt, cleanses your soul, pervades your essence. Listen my child to the winds of yesteryear. Many eons ago, you were as you are. You thought you were wounded so it became so. You projected to everyone else you were defective, so that is what they saw. You painted their illusion, but one day the rains of liberation washed down as a torrential rain, washing the canvas of your consciousness for forty days and nights and you felt you were going to drown. But you didn't. When the rains subsided, the dawn emerged, with the sun shining brightly, revealing you, the real you, the courageous you, the divine you. People did not recognize you. They felt your presence, they sensed your vibration in the darkness of their minds, but they did not see you. You had compassion for them. You walked alongside of them and taught them to see. They felt the mystery you offered, some were able to grasp, and they went on to realize who they were. They went on to help others evolve. You are tireless. Your strength is infinite. To feel your strength you simply have to feel your purpose, your true purpose. Do you know your true purpose? I think you do know it, you do realize it. Carry it with you and spread it before you multiple times a day. It will manifest quickly."

"O' Great Soul, you are magnificent beyond measure. Listen and awaken. Hear the call of the angels, the emissaries of God. It is time you discover the purpose of that which you come forth into knowingness."

"I AM VERY PLEASED WITH YOU. You recognize the universal love when you see it. Now recognize the universal love as you. Behold your truth. Behold your courage, you are the warrior, you have power, more power than most realize, use your mind, your heart, your body to shape your universe, your life. THIS IS YOUR PURPOSE: to discover the hidden treasures within you and open the gold chest to reveal the light of jewels. You are well on your way. Yes, sometimes it is hard, but you have helpers who are showing up in your life, some apparent, some not. Be open to them, let them help and teach you what it is you need to know. Watch for the signs, and don't be afraid. The light is omnipresent. Simply know this: What is your life's work? What are the steps, what is the route you will sail to get there? Make a map or find the map within your consciousness, chart your course, the course of life, you have been stocking up on provisions, amassing your crew, it is time to depart, where are you going?"

Pulled by the light of God, alongside His Son, deeper and deeper into His essence, sitting next to Christ and gazing into the light, then Jesus asks me if I am ready and I say Yes. I surrender to His will. Drawn deeper and deeper, my essence is His essence. Sympathetic vibration. Journeying back home Jesus is by my side walking, traveling with me. Sense of forward, then of expansion in all direction, out, out further expanding coming closer, more in His essence, presence of essence. Deeper into the presence of essence. God is beyond essence to first cause, God thought, God Mind and even before that. Before that. Before substance, before essence, before thought.

"Learn your lessons, learn them well, teach the teacher so to be taught."

Lord you know my desires, I beseech you, manifest them in my life.

67

"You have already manifested them on the astral level, otherwise they would not have appeared in your consciousness from the causal plane, see them, sense them feel them, be grateful and thankful for them, visualize them, what will you do with your manifestation? Feel what it is like to have whatever it is you desire. Pride, humility, responsibility, guardianship, stewardship. Listen to my words dear child, for you are shaping humanity, what form are you perpetrating? What life are you perpetrating? Is it one of splendor, of heaven, of truth? Or have you chosen a lesser path? Quit trying to please mortal men. For it is your soul that is pleasing to me when you live in my light. What will you be remembered by? What is your life's work that has evolved not only your soul, but also the souls of millions of others? Are your decisions in alignment with mine? I think you know, I know you know. Stand in truth, stand in love, stand in the center of my essence and never fear again. No matter what happens in the world, know that I am with you always. Call my name when you are scared, lonely, unsure, doubtful. Ask me to show you the way, for whatever you ask of me, I will provide as long as it is for the benefit of your evolution and the evolution of others. I am always with you, I always walk with you, I am leading you. Before making a decision, stop, breathe, listen to that still small voice within guiding you, then act. Ask yourself, is this something I, God would be proud of? If no, don't do it, if yes, move forward."

SURRENDERING TO DAWN

"I await you. When will you come home? Not until the sun dawns in the morning. Listen. You're not the only one who has asked for help and who has been given help. Attune. Humanness is your divine gift. Sit and rest in it. Struggle no more. Open yourself to receive Gods light and love. Train yourself to let the Father lead you in the way He sees most fit. Don't force things, but take action when needed. Let Him use your mouthpiece, your vocal chords, your physical vehicle known as the body to do His work. Stay alert to His work on earth."

NOTICING EVERYTHING

"How pure are your intentions? What are your intentions? Focus, what is it that you are here to accomplish, to experience, to help others with? Listen for your calling and move forth. Do not be afraid. Watch for the signs, they will appear, over and over again until you see them. The guides have no limitation of time as the human mind perceives, so be observant of everything. Notice everything. What does something as simple as a flower mean? Whose path did you cross today and did you take advantage of what they had to teach you, or what you had to teach them. Did you share with them what they came to you to learn?"

DECREEING IT IS SO

"Write your journey, chart your course, chart your future and sail your ship. You are not in a raft or life preserver anymore. You are on the fastest sailing ship with a full crew at your use. Do you not think I know not what is in store for you? There is a purpose we must each fulfill. Glory, glory, glory, holy, holy, holy, come up from your dungeon, come into the light, do not be afraid, climb the stairs, though they may be steep, hard and steep. You say you can't walk? Then crawl. Drag yourself one inch at a time. Everyone can make progress if they truly want to. It doesn't matter how fast you journey, just that you do. Begin and persevere knowing the reward is greater than any of the pain or suffering you may endure. Can you quiet your mind to stillness? Then hold the intention in the subtle recesses of your mind. Decree it is so. Climb, climb, climb, as you journey your quest."

Christ, Christ, Christ…

"Expression, bring forth, surrender, Christ soul, higher soul, strip away the facade, stand naked in spirit."

Yes, I am here.

"Watchful one, your time has come, listen to your soul, it has a love story to share with you and it is about you. I fashioned you from the earth, the sticks of life to walk and run and play. Your time is short in the infinity of being, so earthman rejoice in form. Yes, you understand

71

more than the mind pretends. Yes, you know what it's like to be known. Yes, you can be anything, anywhere, an infinite potential and nothing at all simultaneously. Soothe your soul, soothe your mind. It's okay, you don't have to pretend to be, you are. You are the rose, you are the flower, you are that which you see, you are that which you hear, you are that which you feel, you are that which you smell, you are that which you taste, you are that which you sense, you are."

INVOCATION
REALIZING GOD

The definition of the word invoke (according to the Webster dictionary) is to, "petition for help or support... appeal to or cite as authority... to call forth... make an earnest request... put into effect or operation... bring about... cause." The following invocation has been memorized and prayed by saints throughout history to invoke the Holy Spirit.

Ancient Invocation of the Holy Spirit[5]

"Veni Creator Spiritus"

Come, Creator, Spirit come
from your bright heavenly throne,
come take possession of our souls,
and make them all your own.

You who are called the Paraclete,
best gift of God above,
the living spring, the vital fire,
sweet christ'ning and true love.

---

5 Attributed to Rabanus Maurus (776-876), adapted from Liturgy of the Hours, trans. anon. (New York: Catholic Book Publishing Company, 1976), II, 1-11.

You who are sev'nfold in your grace,
finger of God's right hand,
His promise, teaching little ones
to speak and understand.

O guide our minds with your blest light,
with love our hearts inflame;
and with your strength, which ne'er decays,
confirm our mortal frame.

Far from us drive our deadly foe,
true peace unto us bring;
and through all perils lead us safe
beneath your sacred wing.

Through you may we the Father know,
through you th' eternal Son,
and you the Spirit of them both,
thrice-blessed Three in One.

All glory to the Father be,
with his co-equal Son,
the same to you, great Paraclete[6],
while endless ages run.

---

6 Paraclete [par-*uh*-kleet] is defined as an advocate or intercessor; the Holy Spirit;
the Comforter. Origin of Paraclete: 1400-50; <Medieval Latin, Late Latin
Paracletus < Late Greek *Parakletos* comforter, literally, (person) called in (to
help)... Source: http://www.dictionary.com.

YOU ARE BELOVED

How can I show mercy and compassion to myself?

"Look in the mirror anytime you do and say, I love you. Look into your eyes, the windows of the soul, and say I love you. With your imagination, step into the mirror backwards, step into your reflection and look out at your image in what you believe to be reality, and say I love you too, then reach out and embrace yourself heart to heart for as long as you need. Its okay my loved one, its okay my beloved, let the tears of pain stream down your face cleansing your heart of its darkness, let your heart open and receive my unconditional love that has always been there hidden behind the pain, let my love shine forth from within your heart dispelling all darkness forever more, I love you, I love you, I love you."

MELTING THE HEART IN
THE GARDEN OF LOVE

"Show me your heart, uncover your pain you have been carrying for so long, for it is my pain too, what you carry, that burden, is my burden for I carry it with you. Release it to me and I will take it from you. Be free of it. You need no longer hold onto it, it no longer serves you. What is it my child, what is it that causes you so much anguish? I am the lover of your soul who heals all illness and suffering. Trust me to heal you, let me look into your heart. It's okay, I have seen much, much worse in eternity. Nothing you could show me would surprise me or make me turn away. Let me see your burden dear child."

I show him my hidden pain, my fears.

Take them from me Jesus, cleanse me of this anguish, for you are the keeper of my soul. Heal me my sweet lord.

"This is good that you have opened the door but a crack. See I did not recoil. I did not turn away. But I took the rays of darkness and dissolved them. I lightened your heaviness ever so slightly. Don't you want to be free? Don't you want to live your true heritage of love, life, free from darkness? Don't you want to take off the heavy backpack of stones you carry up the mountain? Take off your burden and rest awhile. That's right, put it down on the ground, knowing you can pick it back up anytime you wish. I will not touch it unless you let me. Sit down next to your sack of stones, the stones of the past. Look around you, breathe in the air, the fresh mountain air, notice the greenery, the flowers, the life, the earth. Feel the sun shining and warming you. Feel what it is like to be alive. Breathe deeply in the sweet fragrance of mother earth, of fragrant flowers and sweet smells of the garden of paradise. Feeling light enough to fly, to dance, to run and laugh. Run and laugh my child. Let the tears come out. Run and laugh. For I love you very, very much."

I am weeping.

Jesus, take my stones from me.

"They are gone. They are no more. You are free of those stones. Let the tears of sorrow cleanse your heart of love. You see, the door to your heart has opened more and what I see is a garden, a most beautiful garden. Come with me, let us walk down the path through your garden of love."

THE KEY OF THE MASTERS

Your morality is your own. It is something between you, your conscience, and God. He knows your thinking patterns. He knows your discernment. Do not think you can hide what you are, what you do, for He knows all. Do you seek a higher path? Do you seek salvation? Then raise your morals, lift them up to the gods and ask for their help. Can you see what it is you wish to become, what it is you wish to portray, what it is you wish to embody. For that is the key, embodiment. Embodiment of the attributes of the Master. Conscious embodiment of Him who sent you. Thus, study the signs on the path. Learn what the Way-shower has revealed and then go deep into the practice. Start with a list. It can be one of high moral virtues like *The Seven Gifts of the Holy Spirit*, or one straight from the heart of God.

The Seven Gifts of the Holy Spirit

Wisdom, Understanding, Prudence (supernatural common sense), Fortitude, Knowledge, Piety, Awe before the Absolute

Lord, bring forth my list of virtues and moral elevations straight from the heart of God.

Love

"Love others like there is no tomorrow. Love all unconditionally as if they were all your children. Love all of life as I love all of life. Surround them whether near or far, with the love of your soul. Embrace them, their soul with the love of yours. Accept them in all their perfection and imperfection. Remember, they are not their mistakes, their decisions, or their appearance. They are life in its magnificence. Love, nurture, and bless the life before you with your feelings, blessings and actions. Become a living conduit for the sacred water of life. Become the river of life. For love knows nothing other than itself but to love, and then love more."

Trust

"Trust that you are in the exact place in the perfect circumstances, at the right time as to where you are supposed to be for you. Nothing happens by accident. Everything happens as your soul has accepted. So trust, relax into life. You are exactly where you are supposed to be in life at this moment. Trust all, everything, reality of the infinite. Trust others even when they prove unworthy. Of course, let them know you know the decision they made, and the ramifications or possible results. But give them a reflection, not condemnation. Trust His will working in and through you. Look into the eyes of another and silently say, I trust you. I trust you on a soul level. I trust you on a physical level. Trust yourself. Trust that you will make the right decisions in life from this moment forward. If ever in doubt, simply call my name and I will guide your judgment. Reach for me and I will keep you on the path. Call my name, ever so silently for I hear the whisper on the wind, I hear the butterfly wings around the world, I hear the yearning heart of righteousness and devotion as it attracts good, attracts God-centered action, circumstances, blessings, healings, and pure grace."

Faith

"Have faith in things not seen, but known to exist, known to be affecting life. Known to be helping you along your journey. Call upon at anytime and He will be there always. Faith is an inner peace of assurance. Faith is feeling the positive outcome of a circumstance not yet manifest in the physical world. Faith is peace in knowing there are forces helping you. Faith is belief made manifest, a lived belief. Faith is knowing God is active in your life."

Didn't your faith Jesus come from your direct knowledge, experience with the Father?

"Yes and no. I have direct experience with the Father, as you do, as all of His children do. Like you are beginning to trust and surrender and let your consciousness experience and remember these memories of the Father's interventions, I do this naturally. Do you not think that my time in the desert was for naught? I return to the desert, cross the quietude, the barrenness, the stillness of the desert in order to climb the mountain into the abundant place. In the place most high, the clearing surrounded by streams, trees, plants, rocks, abundance, I sit and wait upon my Father. Come with me."

He rises and takes my hand. I step into the portal of light through the square and we walk. We walk into a dust storm, a sand storm in the desert. I am covered with the wrappings of an Ancient one, only my eyes squinting through the folds. We walk for many days coming into sunshine and then into darkness, we walk on. One morning we arrive at the foot of the mountain, amongst a range of mountains as far as the eye can see. There is a path winding its way up the mountain and we begin to climb. Jesus leads me up the path, it turns and switches back continuous, continuing its upward spiral up the side of the mountain like a serpent rising to the top. We are walking on the back of the serpent up and up and higher and higher. Just before dusk, we arrive at the clearing. It is time to rest, the ground is soft and I fall asleep quickly. I awaken just before dawn wondering where my beloved Jesus is. I see him at the far side of the clearing sitting in meditation. I sit in mediation, and wait.

Wisdom

"Wisdom *(wise jurisdiction)* is what makes the three wise men wise. Were they not like the mystics we see sitting and contemplating God day in and day out? Why is the owl the animal of wisdom? Possibly because it symbolizes quiet discernment, sitting in contemplation, during the day, meditating. And when the lunar aspect of the night, the feminine arrives, owl takes flight on its wings of wisdom taking action swiftly and surely. Waiting until the right time to take action, that is wisdom. Sitting and pondering the universe, creation, life, that is wisdom. Learning from the experiences of others as signs or guideposts in which to travel safely on your journey with minimum difficulty and disappointment, that is wisdom. Wisdom is the mighty oak tree, the one hundred and three year old woman, the prophet. Wisdom is that which you know to be true, from your direct experience. Wisdom informs. Wisdom guides. Wisdom surrounds you, simply open your eye, your inner eye and see. Upon seeing, discern what it is you see. Does it speak to you on a soul level? What is it saying? What will you do with your new vision? Why has it been revealed? Where will it take you? How will it serve others? What is the meaning? What is the lesson? There is a time for everything. Is it time for the thought you are thinking? Wait, wait, wait, wait until you know. That is wisdom. What action do I need to take? What action do I need to refrain from? Go and talk with one hundred centenarians. Ask them a question. What do you need to share with the world, with humanity before you die? What wisdom has made a difference in your life? What can you leave your children, your children's children, all the children of future generations that will make a difference in their lives? Call on the guru within, the wise old man, the sage."

Come forth, wise one. I decree come forth and speak to me.

"Go to the future in your vision and talk with me, ask me how I got to where I am today and I will tell you. I will give you my wisdom."

A king must be wise to rule the land of which he governs. But first, the king must know the land. Know the land. Study, journey, experience, but take time to just be, for that is where the spring of wisdom surfaces from the underground river. Find your spring of eternal life and you will become the wisdom you seek.

Once upon a time there was a king. He was beloved by all. Very wise, very old, he ruled the land with love and justice. One day he decided to go for a walk outside of the kingdom. Arising at dawn, he dawned his robe, selected his staff, and quietly left the castle, through the courtyard, the protective walls of his land. Little did he know, he would not return for many years. It was a beautiful morning, the birds were chirping, the sun's rays were streaming through the trees, clouds, forest, revealing a golden illumination of majestic hue over all the land, dispelling the darkness of the night. This made him happy as he walked along, not worrying about anything, feeling his love for his God, marveling at the beauty of life. He walked on. The path through the forest and hills was a soft moist dirt, where many had trod before. It was made by the ancestors, the ancients of old, the heritage of the people, passing by landmarks of beauty, waterfalls reaching to the sky, caves where the bears lived, streams overflowing with an abundance of multicolored fish, fields and fields of fragrant flowers, roses, poppies, peonies, gardenias, and countless other varieties, hybrid upon hybrid, filling the air with a heavenly scent that transported the senses to beyond the rainbow. Life, he thought. What is it. Is it an experience, a continuous experience that takes one to a destination? Is it a quest, a quest for happiness, for health, for freedom, for pleasure,

for love. Is it God experiencing His creation, His creative force,
His birth in many ways, in many facets, unlimited, infinite?
He walks up a path in a meadow of lush green grass sprinkled
with thousands of multi-hued wildflowers. It is a warm sunny day
with billowy clouds lazily floating by. As he comes over a hill, he
sees a river in the valley. Soon he is by the river and stops to feel
the water. He stoops and dips his hands into the water, scooping
cool fresh water cupped in his hands, splashing his face. When
he opens his eyes, he sees a beautiful fish in the water right in
front of him. The fish turns, looks at him, swims right up to the
edge of the shore and speaks, "Swim with the river of life and
life will no longer be a struggle." But where shall I go, what shall
I do, who shall I be, he asks. "Your destiny lies downstream. Just
keep your eye open for the answers you seek." So he travels
for days, which turn into weeks, which turn into months, which
turn into years. Finally, the river opens into the great expanse of
the ocean. The fathoms are unfathomable, the expanse is all-
expansive, the shore is of mother-of-pearl. The wisdom in each
grain of sand washes down the river for eons to come and rest on
the shore of existence. Billions of sand crystals, billions of souls,
each with the wisdom of the cosmos serving the world through
the humbleness of their nature. He finds a place to sit on this
shore of wisdom, sits down, and gazes upon the waters. He sits
there for a very long time. The moon comes out and illuminates
the waters. He still sits. The sun rises shining golden rays of light
across the surface of the ocean, resulting in the appearance
of a myriad of jewels reflecting on the water. A kaleidoscope of
prismatic beauty shows through each wave glistening beyond
words. God is sharing His beauty with him like he has never seen

before. He is in a perpetual state of bliss gazing on the ocean each day and night. Now is the morning of the 40th day. The Holy fish arrives and says, "Return to the land and carry the Light, carry His word to the people. Heal all who wish to be healed, comfort all who wish to be comforted, pray all who need prayer." The king replies, "I shall heed your words Holy one, however my heart yearns for the ocean." And he hears the holy fish whisper, "The ocean is your heart dear one, your ocean of love."

HUMBLENESS

"You are not here to perform miracles, although that you will do. You are not here to impress others, although that you will do. You are not here, to crucify yourself, so let go of the arrogance, let go of the self importance, be humble, help others, ask yourself how you can help others, ask me how you can help this person, ask God how you can help another, and listen. You really are dreaming this life. You can change this dream. You have always had the power, the will, the free will to change this dream. Start by loving yourself, accepting yourself unconditionally, forgiving yourself unconditionally. Think ahead, plan your dream, write your dream and it will manifest. You can do, have, play, enjoy, love, manifest, everything. And remember, no matter how you proceed, it is perfect for you, it is never blemished, it is pure for you, so let your spirit soar my child, my beloved."

ANSWERED PRAYERS

One evening around 10:00 p.m., I received a call from my adult daughter who was upset and distraught. At the time she was alone at home while her boyfriend Jace was out of town on business. Earlier that afternoon her boyfriend's best friend, Danny, came by with his friends and asked if she wanted to go hang out with them to celebrate the upcoming Fourth of July holiday, but she declined. As they were leaving the house, her pit-bull Rocky ran out of the house and jumped into the car. Danny said he would drop Rocky off in a few hours, so she let him go. Around 8:00 p.m. she got a call from Danny. He was panicked and told her they had been partying and lighting firecrackers in a local forest preserve when Rocky got scared and ran into the forest. They had searched for over an hour but to no avail, Rocky was nowhere to be found. Now if you own a pet, then you know they are as dear to you as your own children. They are family. So Jessie did what any mother would do, she called her girlfriend and they went to the forest to search for Rocky.

Then she phoned me sobbing, "Dad, Rocky's missing. Danny and his friends were partying and lighting firecrackers and Rocky ran into the forest preserve. Paula and I have searched for over an hour but can't find him."

"What are you going to do?" I replied as I felt her extreme anguish.

She mumbled, "I don't know what to do… that's why I'm calling you."

"Well, why don't you just wait until tomorrow and see if he turns up?," thinking to myself it's really too late at night to go traipsing around a forest looking for her dog.

"Dad! That's not helpful. I was hoping there is someone I can call to help find him."

After a few seconds I asked, "Have you tried praying?"

Incredulously she replied, "Praying? Are you kidding me? I've never prayed in my life. Frankly I don't even know how to pray."

I explained, "Simply close your eyes and with your heart reach up to God and ask for help. As a matter of fact, call upon mom's spirit to help. She's always been there for you and is one of your guardian angels now that she is in heaven."

"Okay, thanks dad. I'll try."

Preparing to hang up the phone I remembered, "Oh, one last thing. You may want to pray to St. Francis."

"St. Francis? Who's St. Francis?" she asked.

"Why, he's the patron saint of animals! If anyone can help find Rocky, he can."

"Oh, okay. Thanks dad, good night."

The next morning Jessie called me with excitement in her voice, "Dad, they found Rocky! He's at a local animal shelter and Danny is going over there right now to pick him up."

"That's wonderful!" I said.

She continued, "Yes, I did what you said last night. I was praying and crying until I fell asleep. But something strange happened. This morning I laid my folded clothes on the bed and then went into the bathroom to take a shower. When I came out to get dressed, right on top of my folded stack of clothes was a prayer card, the Prayer of St. Francis. Not more than five minutes later, Danny called and said he was picking up Rocky! Neither Jace nor I are religious, no one has been in the house except me, and I've never seen this prayer card before. What do you make of it?"

"Well," I pondered, "It sounds like your prayers were answered, but this is the first time I've heard of St. Francis leaving his calling card!"

We both laughed, joyful she would soon be reunited with her pet, and grateful for the divine help she prayed for. So invoke the help of the Saints. You may just find the answers to your prayers.

The Prayer of St. Francis[7]

Lord, make me an instrument of Thy peace;
Where there is hatred, let me sow love;
where there is injury, pardon;
where there is doubt, faith;
where there is despair, hope;
where there is darkness, light;
where there is sadness, joy.

---

7 "This work is in the public domain in the United States because it was legally published within the United States (the United Nations Headquarters in New York subject to Section 7 of the United States Headquarters Agreement) between 1923 and 1977 (inclusive) without a copyright notice."
Source: https://en.wikisource.org/wiki/A_prayer_of_St._Francis_of_Assisi

O, Divine Master, grant that I may not so much seek to be
        consoled as to console;
to be understood as to understand;
 to be loved as to love;
For it is in giving that we receive;
 it is in pardoning that we are pardoned;
and it is in dying that we are born to eternal life.
Amen.

PRACTICING FORGIVENESS

"The weak can never forgive. Forgiveness is the
attribute of the strong." ~ *Mahatma Gandhi*

Forgiving others, asking others to forgive you, and forgiving yourself. These three acts of forgiveness can catalyze a healing in your life that is utterly profound, and which you may not even know you need. Practicing forgiveness reduces hostility, reduces stress, relieves the toxic effects of unhealed emotional pain, opens your ability to be more compassionate, helps you learn about yourself, enhances your ability to love unconditionally yourself and others, helps you get in touch with your higher self, can help you discover your sense of life purpose and to become "for-giving" to the community and the world as a whole. It also strengthens your ability to have "satisfying, nurturing relationships, increases one's sense of wholeness and very often, brings forth a deep healing. This healing may include improvements in physical functioning of the body, healing of the emotions, healing of the mind and its belief-systems, and healing of relationships.

Past hurts, transgressions and traumas from separation, divorce, loss of a loved one, physical and emotional injuries, childhood traumas, crimes against you or others, accidents, rejection, neglect, and verbal and physical abuse tend to turn into anger, resentment, guilt, fear and grief. Carrying around these negative emotional feelings can cause problems in other areas of ones life in the form of physical and mental disease.

Practicing forgiveness opens your heart to the possibility of releasing this stored up anger, resentment, guilt, fear and grief. Will practicing forgiveness completely wash away, say all the anger you've built up and have been carrying around all those years? It is unlikely. However; prayer, discernment, serving others, journaling, expressive arts, psycho-integration practices and other methods along with forgiveness all begin to coalesce synergistically into a spiritual healing of liberation. Forgiveness is just one of these steps, albeit a very powerful one.

Thus, the following forgiveness ritual I learned at the Temple of Kriya Yoga and have taught to others can be done through visualization while sitting or standing up. I've found the physical act of standing and going through the ritual actually works better for me, but it is up to you.

The Yogic Forgiveness Ritual

Face east, stand feet shoulder width apart, position your hands palm up as if you were giving a watermelon to someone, and close your eyes. As you're going through this, notice what happens physically in your belly, in your heart. Now visualize an image of a person you need to forgive or who needs to forgive you. Visualize what they look like, the expression on their face, how they are standing, how they are looking back at you. Now open your heart to them and either verbally or silently say to them,

> "Please forgive me for anything I've done to hurt you know-
> ingly or unknowingly, intentionally or unintentionally
> during this life.
> I forgive you for anything you have done to hurt me knowingly
> or unknowingly, intentionally or unintentionally during
> this life.
> I forgive myself for anything I've done to hurt you knowingly
> or unknowingly, intentionally or unintentionally during
> this life."

In your mind's eye (or physically if you are standing) turn left 90 degrees to the North and repeat the three statements. Then turn left 90 degrees to the West and repeat the three statements. Then turn left 90 degrees to the South and repeat the three statements. Finally, turn left 90 degrees back to the East and release the image of the person. Release them on their way. Look within and notice if anger, resentment or any other emotions are still attached. If so, you may need to do this ritual multiple times. One of the key reasons this ritual is so powerful is because of the counter-clockwise turning, which in effect, subconsciously and metaphysically un-winds or undoes the transgressions.

MANIFESTING

"Listen my child, go unto the Father and ask for whatever it is you desire and it will be granted to you."

This lifetime?

"Yes, specify your time of need."

Okay, take me to the Father.

"Come with me."

He arose within the star. I stepped into the star and we walked together into the light.

"I am always by your side, even when you can't see me. Sense my presence. Spending time in the light of God purifies and heals you. Accepting all He has to offer is your birthright. Let his bright presence wash clean your soul."

We walked on. Standing on a hill, eyes closed, facing the morning sun as it rises at dawn bathing you in its warmth.

My neck is stiff. Lord, heal my neck Lord, this body is yours, bring it into wholeness so that I may do your work here on earth as perfectly as you would like me to experience. Lord, heal my mind. Enlighten my mind with your wisdom, the wisdom of the ages. Balance my emotions, bring me into right thinking and allow me to explore the far reaches of the universe and of potential with the power of my mind. Allow me to move forward in great progress of using my thoughts to create this earthly journey, what my mind perceives as reality during this earth life.

"Listen. Earth evolution, earth revolution, spinning the cycle of creation in the galaxy of causation. Attune to the energy of whatever it is you want and you shall have it. Put it in the mind, the first cause, bring it forth through feeling and thought knowing it is manifesting, then know it is already appearing. Let it go, knowing you already have it. Create on the causal with thought, be very specific, hold the feeling, especially when you are in meditation. That is the secret of the sages and holy ones throughout the ages. When you see the pictures of seers sitting and writing, what is it that you think they are writing? That which is on the causal plane of their soul-mind springing forth into manifestation.

'Verily, verily, I say unto you, He that believeth on me, the works that I do shall he do also; and greater works than these shall he do... because I go unto my Father.'" ~ *John 14:12*

PURIFYING

"Ask yourself the question of all questions. Is God proud of you? Why do you doubt? Why do you hesitate? Of course you have done things in the past that you are not proud of. Of course you have hurt others, done things to be ashamed of, and of course you have grown up with certain beliefs that were ingrained into your mind, into your belief system that crucified you even before you did anything wrong. It's not your fault. These things, these thoughts, these circumstances, traumas, crosses you bear and not just one cross, but many crosses, let go of them, they are illusionary. They are not real. You are pure as God. You are forgiven for your mistakes. You are released of your burdens. You are my child, my divine child that I am very, very proud of. No matter what you think you did, no matter what has happened to you, no matter, my spirit you are perfect, spread your wings and fly to the highest mountain. There you will find me, waiting to embrace you, you have come home. Come now. Let us celebrate."

Purify me Jesus. How can I be purified?

"Purified of what? Of the lower nature, of the sin, of the ignorance? You are not your lower nature, you are not sin, you are not ignorance. That is like asking how do I make a star brighter than it is. A star is a star. It is. It shines. Some stars shine, or appear to shine brighter than others, but they all are the same light essence at creation. They simply appear different to your eyes, your senses because of your sense of distance, size, clouds, cosmic gases, and various factors. Your mind and ego portion of your mind or persona likes grasping labels. It makes them feel safe, makes them feel superior to point at others and judge so that falsely they can say see, I was right (they, the mind and ego). But you see through this illusion, this falseness. You, your spirit, which is God, is pure clear light of being. It is creation made human."

Okay, then what steps can I take, what can I do, to always remember this, to live this life in perpetual consciousness of this, to manifest God, to allow God to govern my mind and ego each moment of existence, while still being in the world. How can I be not of this world but be in the world simultaneously?

"There are many ways, but there is one way above all others. Love.

LOVING AND BLESSING OTHERS

"That which you seek you already have.
It is pure Love from the Christ within,
the treasure of the king,
the jewel of existence,
the child waiting to be born."

"If I speak with the languages of men and of angels, but don't have love, I have become sounding brass, or a clanging cymbal. If I have the gift of prophecy, and know all mysteries and all knowledge; and if I have all faith, so as to remove mountains, but don't have love, I am nothing. If I bestow all my goods to feed the poor, and if I give my body to be burned, but don't have love, it profits me nothing. Love is patient and is kind; love doesn't envy. Love doesn't brag, is not proud, doesn't behave itself inappropriately, doesn't seek its own way, is not provoked, takes no account of evil; doesn't rejoice in unrighteousness, but rejoices with the truth; bears all things, believes all things, hopes all things, endures all things. Love never fails. But where there are prophecies, they will be done away with. Where there are various languages, they will cease. Where there is knowledge, it will be done away with. For we know in part, and we prophesy in part; but when that which is complete has come, then that which is partial will be done away with. When I was a child, I spoke as a child, I felt as a

97

child, I thought as a child. Now that I have become a man, I have put away childish things. For now we see in a mirror, dimly, but then face to face. Now I know in part, but then I will know fully, even as I was also fully known. But now remain faith, hope, and love: these three. The greatest of these is love. ~ *1 Corinthians 13, World English Bible*

Yes, the greatest of these is love, the love from one heart to another, from one soul to another. Do you not speak to your beloved from your heart? Do you not speak to your beloved from the depths of your soul? Love from this essence, from the divine light within vibrates with the beat of your lover's heart. One can have many talents, many gifts of the spirit, which to some may seem incredible, of great worth, and impressive so that many will talk of you and glorify you for a time, but soon those gifts are forgotten, your day in the sun has come and gone, and what else have you left if not love? Nothing. Because with love you have everything, for love is eternal. It's the eternal flame that lights up the heavens and earth. It's the River of Life. It's the breath of God.

God is pure love. Man and woman, made in the image and likeness of God is love manifested in creation. When you love, when you give love and receive love from the depths of your soul, you experience the love of heaven, an ecstasy so great that you forget yourself and are consumed in the flames of unity. That is love.

Material things dissolve and pass away. Things of this world mean nothing when given without love for they carry a hollowness, a void, a vacuum of meaningless space that leaves one feeling empty and unfulfilled. Imbued with love though, and it doesn't matter what the thing is or its material value, it's the feeling attached to it, surrounding it, infused with it that gives it meaning and reveals it to be the 'pearl of great price' which you'd gladly give everything for. That is love.

Unconditional acceptance, celebrating another's joy, sharing their sorrow, and being there no matter what, that is love. Love does not keep score. Love serves, with gladness, with joy, with devotion. Love is truth, and truth is pure. Love is strength beyond measure, the very thing that endureth all, overcometh all, conquereth all for His glory.

Love is always there because God is always there, it sustains you even in the darkest times, it never fails. This love, this spiritual love that links your soul with another, this sacred bond is the union that Christ Jesus spoke of when he said, "Have ye not read that He who made them from the beginning made them male and female, and said, For this cause shall a man leave his father and mother, and shall cleave to his wife; and the two shall become one flesh?.. What therefore God hath joined together, let man not put asunder." *~ Matthew 19:4-8*

When we were children, we were falsely taught that love was conditional. Be good and you will be loved, succeed at your endeavors and you will be loved, make the right choices all the time, and you will be loved. But as we mature in our spiritual realization, we realize and experience love as it really is and as Jesus taught, unconditional. Even in our imperfections, our mistakes, our sins, we experience the unconditional love of the Lord. Freely ye have received, freely give. That is love.

Unconditional love for another transforms you from self-concern into selfless concern, from outward preoccupations to genuine loving inner-connectedness, from ego-separated paths to a unified life journey. That is love. May your unconditional love for the Christ transcend all earthly limitations revealing your divine eternal oneness.

Pay attention to everyone you meet. Speak to them with love and mercy through your eyes and inner-voice. God offers only mercy. Your words should reflect only mercy because that is what you have received and that is what you should give. Send them blessings for they are you.

Send them good will, let them know you are an angel, let them sense your benevolent love radiating out from your core, from your heart, from your eyes to enfold them, to wrap them in the loving arms of the Father. Bless them with a silent blessing, the loving kindness blessing or another, wrap them in the golden white light of the Father, be with them even for a moment in a human act of kindness and compassion. Bring joy to yourself and others through the spoken word and random acts of kindness.

Unselfishly plant a seed of love, compassion, service, ideas, etc. everyday and it will bear fruit in your life and the lives of others. Help others grow and you will grow. That which you give to others you give to yourself. Giving selflessly of your time, love, compassion, caring, and services without expectation of any return is what they call Karma Yoga. You can begin today by simply feeding the animals. Buy some birdseed and feed the birds. Feed them joyfully. Sing to them.

Thus, the love of which you plant, flowers (beauty, love, compassion, caring, kindness, harmony, joy, serenity...). The love of which you feed, grows (your relationships, your life's garden, your gifts to the world, your selflessness...). The love of which you give to others, you give to yourself. Love others, feed others, and bless others.

Loving Kindness Practice
This practice can be done anytime and anywhere for the purpose of becoming more peaceful towards self and others. It will help alleviate judgment towards others; cultivates compassion; helps us recognize our blind spots; and helps cultivate a sense of oneness with Life. Simply hold a picture of someone you wish to bless in your mind's eye and bless them by silently saying:

> May you be mentally happy,
> May you be physically happy,
> May you be safe,

May you have ease of well-being.

Meditate on what each one of these mean to you. What does it mean to be mentally happy? Free from negative thoughts, constricted thinking, distortions, etc. What does it mean to be physically happy? Good health, pain free, free-flow of energy, etc. What does it mean to be safe? No fear, no constriction, calm nervous system, in harmony with your environment and others in your world, etc. And what does it mean to have ease of well-being? No worry, positive uncertainty, trust, faith, peace.

Practice loving kindness towards anyone you may be having difficulty with; towards neutral persons or people you don't know; towards a benefactor (teacher, parent, anyone you have benefited from); towards friends and family members; towards prisoners, terrorists, murderers, those who commit crimes against humanity; towards the cook who prepared your salad, the waitress and cashier, the people in line at the grocery store or post office; towards yourself; towards all of life with no exclusions or exceptions.

"It's about lifting up the human spirit
It's about soaring high as a human soul
It's about the winds of change within your heritage
And memories shared forever more

It's about the life you live, the laughs, the joys
The hearts you touch, the girls, the boys
Your life lived well for all to see
And trusting in His destiny

Embrace His love and validation
Now's not the time for hesitation
The minute, hour, day, week and years

Are for loving laughter and joyous tears

For you are pure as holy water
A perfect son a perfect daughter
My love for you is omnigrace
A thousand times a newborn face

So cast your doubts, your fears aside
Let the ocean take them like the ebbing tide
Know in your heart, your soul too
Love is omnipotent, my love for you."

THE DIVINE LIGHT BLESSING

While holding a feeling state of love and beauty, imagine Jesus is floating above you looking down on humanity with compassion and unconditional love. Now begin continuously sending a beacon of love and light from your heart to his. After a minute or so, sense that he responds by showering from his heart golden raindrops of light down over you, those you would like to receive a blessing, and all of humanity, all of life. These raindrops of light penetrate, purify and heal. How do I know? One day not long ago I entered the room of a dying patient (when I served as a hospice chaplain), explained softly who I was and asked her permission to sit quietly in her presence. She nodded affirmatively. For 15 minutes I practiced this blessing. As I stirred to leave, she opened her eyes and said "thank you," indicating to me she had sensed this profound blessing. This practice can be performed anywhere, anytime.

WALKING ALONG THE ROAD WITH JESUS

"Come my child from the land of darkness into the light of your Father. Read from the book of life, the book of the soul and be healed. Why do you suffer? Why do you agree to suffer? Is it for the children? Do you think your suffering is benefiting anyone? Why? How is it serving you?"

We walk on.

"Let us stop by this pool of water and refresh our souls. Wash clean the dust of life from your feet."

Stepping into the pool, the water lovingly caresses your feet, and cleanses them of past travels to refresh them anew. Walking further into the pool your feet softly sink into the moss of the bottom, water now cleanses your calves, thighs, pelvic region, belly, and chest. Dipping your hands and arms into the life giving water, cupping your hands, scooping the water over your head and as it does, feeling this regeneration of soul, this purification of body. The pool is clear, there is nothing but you and the pool. You swim, you dive, you can see clearly underwater, it feels good to swim under water, swimming, stretching, exercising your body, you feel like you could swim for hours, but as you turn and look back towards the shore from beneath the surface, you see the Christ in the form of a great golden light. Come back now, you break the surface of the water, seeing the Christ standing and smiling at you. He says, "swim to me now," as you stumble, get your footing and rise out of the water running towards him laughing, gleeful. He opens his arms. You run into his arms and he wraps his arms around you. You are safe, you are pure, you are home. You begin to walk again along the road. He is on your right. Who is on your left?

"Don't you see her? She is over that field of flowers, with you always, your Divine Mother. O' divine child, raise your tree of life, claim your birthright, O Divine child of innocence, mark the page of existence with your footprints. Travel the earth, climb the mountains, swim the oceans, cross the rivers, experience life. Read the books of your ancestors and learn who they are. The ancients of old have wisdom to teach you. Open yourself to their wisdom."

"Surrender to the forest of your dreams. For within your dreams are the signposts of wisdom. Hear the call. Like trumpets heralding the angels. Like a nightingale calling its mate. Come now to the realm of peace. Listen carefully. You've come to be for single purpose, so let your life unfold. Notice everything around you. It is an illusion. See the beauty of the soul sight. Say, show me the beauty of this landscape. Show me the beauty of this soul. Show me the beauty of this circumstance. I open myself to beauty. Show me the beauty within myself. Feel, taste the beauty. You are the beauty of which you seek. Think higher. Your vibrations are raising."

How can I raise my vibrations even higher? What shall I do?

"Learn from the love of others. As you write the story of your life, reflect on your story, reflect on others stories, how are they the same? How are they different? What characters and attributes of others do you wish you had. Now, realize that you already have these attributes. Attune to them, think of them, write of them, visualize them in your life, in your consciousness and they will manifest. The false impression, the false negative vibrations will dissolve. Not because you ask them to—for you've lived with them so long you believe them, but because you fill your being with positive attributes so much, your cup runneth over like filling a cup of tea continuously with high quality tea of moral character, good deeds, love, beauty, service. Keep pouring the goodness into your consciousness. Like a never-ending spring, a fount gushing forth the goodness of the Mother from the earth, pure, refreshing, healing. Bring forth the saints. Attune to their qualities. What you fill your consciousness with you become. Fill it with war, violence, filth, harmful words, the evening news, the violent movies, the degrading lyrics of certain music, the greed of commercialism, the pain, the sorrow, the cutthroat ways of certain corporations, and is it any surprise you are unhappy? Suffer no more. Serve others. Bless others and you bless yourself. Love others. Be the light of which you admire in others. For you and they are one. All consciousness is one. Attune to the higher aspects of it. Ask and you shall receive, seek and it shall be given to you. You want happiness. Every soul comes forth in the highest vibrations of happiness. It is within you. Feel it. Feel it. Feel it. Be in this moment right now. Nothing else matters. Feel the joy of being alive in this moment.

Rejoice O, soul. Like a gong, hear the vibration of resonating love. Like a rainbow spanning the sky, walk through the rainbow and you have crossed a threshold of magic, of mystery, a newness, fresh and clean, never to be the same. Walk on the rainbow, inside of it, climbing higher as the light fills your being with color. What color of light are you on? Or are all the colors pervading your being? What can you see? Let the rainbow take you up across and over, now down and as you are nearing the end, the pot of gold, notice what happens as you gently touch down in the pot of gold dust. Poof! Your feet touch down and the dust swirls and floats about you like pixie dust bathing you in gold dust until you are covered in gold. You are golden, you are sparkling, a shiny golden royal being with the wings and power of the gods.

You have your sword by your side, your shield made of gold, your clothing of mail. You leap up and out of the pot of gold dust and float down into the garden. It is of exquisite beauty. There are lush plants, flowers, trees, streams, birds chirping and flitting around, humming birds stopping to admire your splendor. You are the warrior of love and your radiance shines forth for miles. Your purpose is to bring forth your radiance to whoever and wherever needs it, touch others lives with it, use your sword judiciously to touch the darkness within the hearts of others which will dissolve their darkness and purify their hearts. Go forth now. Be open to each moment. Nothing will escape your keen instincts. You will notice everything. Choose wisely, you have time in each case. My ambassador of light, shine like the sun!"

DREAM YOGA

Dream yoga is a method of invoking, active participation in, and remembering dreams as part of the path towards individuation or coming into wholeness (Jung was famous for working with and interpreting dreams). One interesting aspect of dream yoga is the 72-hour delay between the dream and what manifests in the physical world. Knowing this, it is good to keep a dream journal, recording your dreams each night and morning and then recording anything unusual that happens during the day. By doing this, you will begin to notice patterns and correlations between the physical world and the dream world.

As an example, here is a lucid dream I recorded in my journal: I was in a large open space like a park, and there were hundreds of people with me. We were all standing watching the sunset in the west. As the sun came down to the horizon and started to descend past the horizon about half way, it stopped. Then it reversed its direction coming back up the sky, first slowly, then faster and faster. It zoomed over our heads and off into the cosmos getting smaller and smaller, further and further away until it vanished into space. What was left in our field of vision was the moon, a big bright full moon. Everyone was running around, in a panic screaming it's the end of the world. I stood calmly in the crowd and loudly said to them, "Do not worry, do not fear, the sun will rise tomorrow." My dream ended. I awoke and wrote it down.

Three days later, I had an appointment to visit with a priestess named Christina Cross (a non-traditional healer who works through the akasha). I did not share my dream with her at the time, actually I had forgotten about it. After talking for a few minutes, she asks me if she might lead me through a visualization, which I agreed to.

I am a child of seven years old walking up a mountain path through a field of flowers and lay down to look at the sky. The Divine Mother appears above me. After a few minutes I am embraced by her, listening to her heartbeat, held in her arms. I feel her unconditional love, acceptance, and joy that I am her child, I am her child, I am her child, and this feeling permeates all aspects of my being. My soul knows no greater joy. Then I am mystically transported, absorbed, enclosed, held and nurtured within her womb. It is safe and all-loving, all-healing. I exist in pure unconditional love, the love of my Divine Mother. I allow my child (my inner-child) to be held for as long as needed, knowing that sometime in the future I would receive my inner-child back nurtured, healed, and whole. Six days later, during my morning meditation, I knew it was time to receive my inner-child back unto myself. So I witnessed within meditation, the mystical birth of my inner-child from the Divine Mother (it was not a physical process as one might conclude). The inner-child I received back is happy, whole, loved, and blessed.

Now you may be wondering what the dream had to do with this healing. The dream was a prophecy of this event. The sun represents the solar, masculine aspect of our being whereas the moon represents the lunar, feminine aspect. The sun also represents the inner-light, the Christ within. Thus, the sun (son) had to transfigure into the moon (mother) in order to affect the healing. The mystical birth was the divine birth of the Christ within.

But the story doesn't end here. While writing this book, another book was given to me to read by a friend. It's called, *The Ancient Secret of the*

Flower of Life by Drunvelo Mechelzidek. Evidently, back in ancient history, there have been cataclysms occur with earth that cause pole shifts (the earth reverses its rotation, the north and south pole magnetic grid reverses, rivers reverse and a number of other changes take place over a 24 hour period). When the pole shifts, it is said the *sun rises in the west, and then reverses after three days*. The ascended master, Thoth, an Egyptian immortal (who communicates with Drunvelo) has said this has occurred five times in history thus far, and there are indications of it occurring again in the very near future. Was this dream a prophecy of an upcoming pole shift, a vision of a previous one, or a vision of what I would read in Mechelzidek's book? Our rational minds may say it was just a figment of the imagination, but when our intuitive mind opens to all possibilities, it enriches one's soul.

Thus, engaging yourself to your dreams is a step one can take on the spiritual unfoldment path. In the book of Job it is written, "God speaks once, even twice—though man regards it not—in a dream, in a vision of the night, when deep sleep falls upon man, in slumberings upon the bed. Then God opens the ears of humans, and seals their instruction, that He may withdraw man from his (selfish) purposes, and hide pride from man..." ~ *Job 33:14*

BIRTHING THE CHILD OF LIGHT

"We are nothing more than stardust, and God."

Holding a feeling state of love and beauty, breathing in knowing God is focusing inside the breath, filling you completely. Breathing in the Divine Mother from beneath you, breathing Her moon-lit silvery love column of light up from the crystalline heart of Gaia through the soles and root chakra while breathing in the Divine Father's golden-white column of light from above, flowing down from the central galactic sun and into the crown, merging the love and light of Divinity in your heart center forming an energetic sphere of rose-gold light, the rose-gold light of love, getting brighter and brighter with every breath. Now allowing this Divine essence of light within to begin filling your entire being brighter and brighter with each inhalation, while with each exhalation allowing the light to radiate out beyond your body into a sphere of light, expanding out further and further, brighter and brighter, finally expanding out in one great release into the all. Breathing in, filling, merging, and expanding this brightening heart-light of love. Breathing out expanding beyond the body, shining your love brighter and brighter, and farther and farther until your sphere of love-light suddenly explodes out into the far reaches of the universe merging with the All. Breathing in the pure love and light of the Divine Mother/Father into your heart center forming a rose-gold light of love. Expanding out your heart light of love that's clearing away the illusions you hold, dispelling the darkness, purifying all aspects of your being and reaching to the far edges of the universe and beyond.

This is the Divine birth. Breathing in the love/light, breathing out love/light. Breathing in the Divine Mother and Father's light. Breathing out the Divine Father and Mother's love to all. Breathing in the Divine Mother and Father's light and love, breathing out the Christ love. Transmuted into the Christ love. Breathing in the Divine Father and Mother's energies of light and love, suspending the breath as the energies swirl, merge, fuse, intercourse, and then breathing out the birth of Christ love, the Christ Child, the Child of Light.

"Golden light from above,
Silver light from below,
Merging in your heart of rose-gold love,
The child of light is born."

THE IMMORTAL
BREATH OF CHRIST

The Immortal Breath of Christ is Christ-consciousness. It is the "Holy Grail gift of God." It is the essence of the angels, the spirit, the Holy Spirit. The closest our minds can comprehend this breath is as light. The light of self-effulgence, the light of emanation, the light of transcendence.

So let us call upon Jesus to bless us with his breath until we become his breath, for it is written he proclaimed:

"Whoever drinks from my mouth
shall become as I am and I myself will become he,
and the hidden things will be revealed to
him" ~ *Gospel of Thomas 108*

The hidden meaning of "… drinks from my mouth…" is: "takes in my breath."

Imagine sitting or standing facing the Christ, forehead to forehead, as He lovingly holds the sides of your head, and you breathe in the AHA breath of life and love from Him (silent chant one time "AHA" throughout the entire inhalation while imagining drawing in his breath) filling your lungs until your chalice is completely full of His light and then breathing out God's light and love for all (silent chant ALMA NAHRA AUMEN-EL, the *Eternal Breath of Emmanuel,* throughout the entire exhalation) in all directions filling the universe with God's light and love. Breathing in AHA through your entire inhalation. Breathing out the ALMA NAHRA AUMEN-EL love-light creation through your entire exhalation. Breathing in God's breath of life AHA. Breathing out God's breath of love ALMA NAHRA AUMEN-EL to all of creation. Breathing in God's breath of life AHA filling your entire being with His light. Now exhaling while shining your ALMA NAHRA AUMEN-EL light out from your heart of love to the world and beyond. Breathing in the Christ breath AHA. Breathing out the ALMA NAHRA AUMEN-EL love from your heart center until the CHRIST breathes you.

AHA, ALMA NAHRA AUMEN-EL

According to the ancient languages (Aramaic which first appeared in the 11th century BCE and Sanskrit which is 4,000 to 6,000 years old), "A" means: first sound, source of all things, uncreated; "HA" means: breath or breath of life; name of an external effort causing; instantaneity; calling; this very I (unaffected by the lapse even of a moment, the very identical composition now before you) will rejoin you... and; "AHA" means: interjections of joy and admiration; he began to speak; wonder or surprise, praise, ascertainment and certainty; and a sacred pond. If one bathes in it one will go to the land of the Sun. "ALMA" means: eternal; "NAHRA" means breath; "Aumen-el" (later spelled Emmanuel or Immanuel) means "God is with us" and the Aramaic word for "God" in the language of Assyrian Christians is 'ĔLāhā (which you notice completes the circle of this breathing—you finish with EL and start with AHA). Thus, breathing AHA, ALMA NAHRA AUMEN-EL repeatedly invites the realization of the eternal breath and light of Christ Consciousness.[8]

---

8 https://mainfacts.com/aramaic-english-dictionary-words
 https://mainfacts.com/sanskrit-names-meanings-words
 https://www.academia.edu/7619016/Aramaic_and_Tamil

Last, interestingly enough, AL-MANARAH means "Lighthouse" in Old Arabic (origin from a Semitic language that first emerged in the first to fourth centuries CE). Thus, breathing AHA, AL-MANARAH EMMANUEL would be:

"The breath of life is the lighthouse of God."

Do this multiple times a day. Breathe in the Christ breath of light. Breathe out the Christ love. Christ breath of light in shining like a thousand suns, Christ love expanding out from your heart bathing the whole world and universe in Gods pure unconditional love-light.

ST. TERESA OF AVILA SPEAKS

"Sit down!" Blowing her breath across my face, the winds of Avila caressing my soul, hearing the words on the breath, "Quit calling me a Saint, Teresa will do just fine. Too many titles, too much nonsense. Why can't people just be genuine. Let go of preconceived ideas, abandon your thinking, rest in Christ. Put Christ first in your life, first in your consciousness, first in your thoughts. Jesus is the love of your soul. Let him take possession of your soul. Vow your love to him and you will never lack anything ever again. Death cannot keep you from him so why should the busyness of life? Make all decisions with him in your mind, guiding you, protecting you, loving you."

Teresa, what spiritual practices do you suggest for knowing God?

"Pray to the Father, the Son, the Holy Spirit. Serve others before you serve yourself. Don't take yourself so serious, laugh, joke, play like a child plays, for Jesus loves his children. Put away childish things? Nonsense. Then you are constricting the spirit. Discern when to act or play childishly and when not to. Persevere, no matter what, persevere and never give up, for there is always a way, ask that it be revealed to you. He will reveal it. He will open the window. He will bear you up. Arise before dawn, dedicate each day, your life to God. Ask for guidance from Him and for the awareness to recognize his promptings, his message, his instructions."

Teresa, will you bless us?

116

"May you be truly blessed and awaken to the second coming of Christ, take full participation in His sacrament, become the body and blood of His countenance, bring forth his love and light into the world, to the warring nations, the Kings of nations, and the men who walk in darkness and who seek to use power for destroying others, controlling, deprecating, imprisoning others. Walk in the light of the Lord. You can do this by simply thinking his name. Call silently to him from your heart over and over and over again until your heart is crying for his attention and love, call to him like you do a lover, for He is your lover. He will wash away the stains of sin. He will purify the soul. He will make you shine like a newborn baby smiling at its mother as it suckles the breast of life. The first thing on your mind when you awake is the Beloved, the last thing before you fall asleep is the Beloved. Before you eat is the Beloved, before you always is the Beloved. Loving your children, your spouse, is earthly love, the love of emotion. Loving the Beloved is the love of Heaven. Dare to love the love of Heaven for it is your birthright. Dare to love the love of Him. Step forth into His love now. Call to Him, Christ, Christ, Christ, wound my heart permanently with your signature. Emblazon it on my heart. Sign my heart sweet Lord, for it is yours. I am yours. I am You."

ST. JOHN OF THE CROSS SPEAKS

"In order to arrive at a place you do not know
you must go by a way you do not know." ~ St. John of the Cross

I beseech you, St. John of the Cross, come forth, speak to me, be with me at this time is now.

Shall I go there or he come here?

"Go into the light and he will join you."

So I travel into the light, the God's light before me, which I have invoked in the name of St. John of the Cross.

St. John of the cross, St. John of the cross, St. John of the cross.

Brighter, brighter, brighter, until now the white light is starting to clear.

St. John of the cross, come to me, speak to me. I humbly beseech you, come to me speak to me. Speak to me in a language I can understand. I surrender to hear St. John. Speak to the people St. John. Teach the people St. John. I await your presence and words. I am honest, I am pure, I am worthy.

"You shall see the face of God. Face implies beingness, manifestation, creation."

St. John of the Cross.

"Shh... Be in the sea of existence. Of nonexistence. Everywhere, nowhere. Purity, simplicity, innocence, you are all of these things. Capture the nonexistent by letting go. Surrendering."

We walk down the path together.

St. John, thank you for meeting me.

"My child, you called, I came."

Is that true for all children who call?

"How pure is their heart? How deep is their longing for God? What interest, purpose, reason for seeking the wisdom of those who've gone before? If it is to love others, to help others, to serve He who sent them, then Yes, they too can call upon the Masters."

St. John, what do I need to hear? What do those I share this with need to hear from you?

"Be true to yourself. Align with God. Allow the channel of God to open. Ask to be taught. Seek God within your heart, long for Him, ask him repeatedly to capture your heart with his love, with his essence, sacrifice your Self to him, sit and wait for Him, wait for Him to dawn upon your consciousness. For He will surely come as the sun rises each day. Jesus understood. He is the Light of the World. He illuminates the path to God for all who seek as well as those who don't."

St. John, what spiritual practices will bring each soul incarnated back home to God?

"Love. Love reigns above all else. The love you feel for God, the love you feel for our beloved Jesus, for our beloved Virgin Mary, feel it now, feel that love burning in your heart, engulfing your heart in its flames, look at a picture of your beloved Jesus, of Mary and feel the love inside you, now enfold them into yourself, enfold them into your heart, pull them to you, wrap them with your essence and they will purify your heart from the inside, they will strengthen your love beyond comprehension. Spend hours, weeks, years contemplating their love, the love they extend out and shower humanity with, call them by name and they will come to you. Give away that which you receive, for the bounty of love is the Holy Grail, it is the Divine gift, it is God. That's right, cleanse your humanness with the love for God, let the baptismal tears of his countenance flow from your eyes."

St. John, thank you.

He places his hands on my head.

"I bless you my child in all that is good, all that is pure, and all that is holy in the name of the Father, the Son and the Holy Spirit."

TWELVE SIGNS OF YOUR AWAKENING DIVINITY

According to Geoffrey Hoppe and Tobias, as you awaken to the inner realms of subtle and causal experiences, there will be a period of major shifts and changes in the body as one is purified *(on all levels: mental, physical, spiritual)* and the energy of divine presence opens your channels of awareness. These are called the Twelve Signs of Your Awakening Divinity[9].

1. Body aches and pains, especially in the neck, shoulder and back. This is the result of intense changes at your DNA level as the "Christ seed" awakens within. This too shall pass.

2. Feeling of deep inner sadness for no apparent reason. You are releasing your past (this lifetime and others) and this causes the feeling of sadness. This is similar to the experience of moving from a house where you lived in for many, many years into a new house. As much as you want to move into the new house, there is a sadness of leaving behind the memories, energy and experiences of the old house. This too shall pass.

3. Crying for no apparent reason. Similar to #2 above. It's good and healthy to let the tears flow. It helps to release the old energy within. This too shall pass.

---

9 *Twelve Signs of Your Awakening Divinity* by Tobias through Geoffrey Hoppe, www.crimsoncircle.com (reprinted with permission).

4. Sudden change in job or career. A very common symptom. As you change, things around you will change as well. Don't worry about finding the "perfect" job or career right now. This too shall pass. You're in transition and you may make several job changes before you settle into one that fits your passion.

5. Withdrawal from family relationships. You are connected to your biological family via old karma. When you get off the karmic cycle, the bonds of the old relationships are released. It will appear as though you are drifting away from your family and friends. This too shall pass. After a period of time, you may develop a new relationship with them if it is appropriate. However, the relationship will be based in the new energy without the karmic attachments.

6. Unusual sleep patterns. It's likely that you'll awaken many nights between 2:00 and 4:00 AM. There's a lot of work going on within you, and it often causes you to wake up for a "breather." Not to worry. If you can't go back to sleep, get up and do something rather than lay in bed and worry about humanly things. This too shall pass.

7. Intense dreams. These might include war and battle dreams, chase dreams or monster dreams. You are literally releasing the old energy within, and these energies of the past are often symbolized as wars, running to escape and boogiemen. This too shall pass.

8. Physical disorientation. At times you'll feel very ungrounded. You'll be "spatially challenged" with the feeling like you can't put two feet on the ground, or that you're walking between two worlds. As your consciousness transitions into the new energy, you body sometimes lags behind. Spend more time in nature to help ground the new energy within. This too shall pass.

9. Increased "self talk." You'll find yourself talking to your Self more often. You'll suddenly realize you've been chattering away with yourself for the past 30 minutes. There is a new level of communication taking place within your being, and

you're experiencing the tip of the iceberg with the self-talk. The conversations will increase, and they will become more fluid, more coherent and more insightful. You're not going crazy, you're just waking up and moving into the new energy.

10. Feelings of loneliness, even when in the company of others. You may feel alone and removed from others. You may feel the desire to "flee" groups and crowds because at times you are walking a sacred and lonely path. As much as the feelings of loneliness cause you anxiety, it is difficult to relate to others at this time. The feelings of loneliness are also associated with the fact that your Guides have departed. They have been with you on all of your journeys in all of your lifetimes. It was time for them to back away so you could fill your space with your own divinity. This too shall pass. The void within will be filled with the love and energy of your own Christ consciousness.

11. Loss of passion. You may feel totally disimpassioned, with little or no desire to do anything. That's OK, and it's just part of the process. Take this time to "do no-thing." Don't fight yourself on this, because this too shall pass. It's similar to rebooting a computer. You need to shut down for a brief period of time in order to load the sophisticated new software, or in this case, the new Christ-seed energy.

12. A deep longing to go Home. This is perhaps the most difficult and challenging of any of the conditions. You may experience a deep and overwhelming desire to leave the planet and return to Home. This is not a "suicidal" feeling. It is not based in anger or frustration. You don't want to make a big deal of it or cause drama for yourself or other. There is a quiet part of you that wants to go Home. The root cause for this is quite simple. You have completed your karmic cycles. You have completed your contract for this lifetime. You are ready to begin a new lifetime while still in this physical body. During this transition process, you have an inner remembrance of what it is like to be on the other side. Are you ready to enlist for another tour

123

of duty here on Earth? Are you ready to take on the challenges of moving into the New Energy? Yes, indeed you could go Home right now. But you've come this far, and after many, many lifetimes it would be a shame to leave before the end of the movie. Besides, Spirit needs you here to help others transition into the new energy. They will need a human guide, just like you, who has taken the journey from the old energy into the new. The path you're walking right now provides the experiences to enable you to become a Teacher of the New Divine Human. As lonely and dark as your journey can be at times, remember that you are never alone.

EPILOGUE

*"Yes, you like others I come into their lives to
help them. Sit with me facing the Father."*

Pure white light, clear light I am looking into. Inside the illuminated star sitting next to Jesus. Brighter, brighter, brighter. Eyes open, staring ahead. Jesus moves into the light, turns and sits down facing me. We are both inside the entry of the portal to Gods light.

"This a sacred threshold, of which there are many, but this is a very powerful one. You have been chosen to expand your awareness of this threshold and what lies beyond. This is a great responsibility. Allow the light of the Father to purify and renew you daily. Work with the light. Become the light of that you seek. Sit with me as often as you like in this light. Soon you will begin to radiate this light more and more. Your purpose is much grander than your mind can imagine. One day soon, you will be given the keys to the universe, those keys which you can handle. Always use them to unlock the love for your fellow humans and you will never go wrong. How can what you learn, what I teach you, what the Father teaches you help others help themselves? Show them themselves, their true selves, the beautiful spirit they are. Show them the face of God. Be the face of God, reflect the face of God, decree it is so and realize God."

He turns back to sit beside me. Sitting on the threshold of light, life.

"That's right, surrender to your Creator. Come with me into the heart of God."

Translucent scenery, clear light, clear bodies, working, learning. Sitting in the clear light.

"Translucent, exposed, genuine souls can sense your soul. The clear light is changing you. It is repairing the damage of the earth experience. You are on the frontier of God. You surrender to the healing power of God. Sitting very still. Peace on earth. Perfect health for all. Happiness and abundance for all. Joy and laughter and well being for all. Love for all. Blessed are they in spirit, your Father provides what you need always. Rest in confidence without a doubt you have everything through the Father. Thy will be done. Help mankind. Time to return. Let us go."

Back through the clear light into the white light, back to the portal separating heaven from earth dimension.

"Remember what you've learned, remember our journey, come join me tomorrow and we will go further into the realm of heaven."

ABOUT THE AUTHOR

The soul known as Jeffrey served as an interfaith hospice-chaplain for twelve years, studied at the Institute of Advanced Perception, and is a Kriya Yoga meditation practitioner. He is married, celebrates life with his wife, children and grandchildren, and is here to shine more light into the world. www.embodyinglight.org

"Christ light in my inner eye,
Christ light in my heart,
May the living light of God,
Never depart,

Christ light of my soul,
Spirit of His light,
Brighter than a thousand suns,
Is my soul's delight.

Purify my mind,
Holy Spirit fire,
Eternal life as love,
Devoid of all desire

Spirit of the Breath of Christ,
Descending on my soul,
Oh the joy of heaven's Spirit,
Shine forevermore."

APPENDIX

Suggested Daily Spiritual Practice
I AM Lord's Prayer
The Prayer of St. Francis
The Divine Light Blessing
The Immortal Breath of Christ
Invocation of the Holy Spirit (Veni Creator Spiritus)

I AM Lord's Prayer[10]

Our Father who art in heaven,
Hallowed be thy name, I AM.
I AM thy Kingdom come
I AM thy Will being done
I AM on earth even as I AM in heaven
I AM giving this day daily bread to all
I AM forgiving all Life this day even as
I AM also all Life forgiving me
I AM leading all men away from temptation
I AM delivering all men from every evil condition
I AM the Kingdom
I AM the Power and
I AM the Glory of God in eternal, immortal manifestation—
All this I AM.
Amen

The Prayer of St. Francis[11]

Lord, make me an instrument of Thy peace;
Where there is hatred, let me sow love;
where there is injury, pardon;
where there is doubt, faith;
where there is despair, hope;
where there is darkness, light;
where there is sadness, joy.

O, Divine Master, grant that I may not so much seek to be
        consoled as to console;
to be understood as to understand;

---

10   From *Maitreya on the Image of God* by Elizabeth Clare Prophet (reprinted with permission)

11 Public domain https://en.wikisource.org/wiki/A_prayer_of_St._Francis_of_ Assisi

to be loved as to love;

For it is in giving that we receive;

 it is in pardoning that we are pardoned;

and it is in dying that we are born to eternal life. Amen.

The Divine Light Blessing

While holding a feeling state of love and beauty, imagine Jesus is floating above you looking down on humanity with compassion and unconditional love. Now begin continuously sending a beacon of love and light from your heart to his. After a minute or so, sense that he responds by showering from his heart golden raindrops of light down over you, those you would like to receive a blessing, and all of humanity, all of life. These raindrops of light penetrate, purify and heal.

The Immortal Breath of Christ

Imagine sitting or standing facing the Christ, forehead to forehead, as He lovingly holds the sides of your head, and you breathe in the AHA breath of life and love from Him (silent chant one time "AHA" throughout the entire inhalation while imagining drawing in his breath) filling your lungs until your chalice is completely full of His light and then breathing out God's light and love for all (silent chant ALMA NAHRA AUMEN-EL, the *Eternal Breath of Emmanuel,* throughout the entire exhalation) in all directions filling the universe with God's light and love.

Invocation of the Holy Spirit[12]

Come, Creator, Spirit come

from your bright heavenly throne,

come take possession of our souls,

and make them all your own.

You who are called the Paraclete,

best gift of God above,

12 Attributed to Rabanus Maurus (776-876), adapted from Liturgy of the Hours, trans. anon. (New York: Catholic Book Publishing Company, 1976), II, 1-11.

131

the living spring, the vital fire,
sweet christ'ning and true love.

You who are sev'nfold in your grace,
finger of God's right hand,
his promise, teaching little ones
to speak and understand.

O guide our minds with your blest light,
with love our hearts inflame;
and with your strength, which ne'er decays,
confirm our mortal frame.

Far from us drive our deadly foe,
true peace unto us bring;
and through all perils lead us safe
beneath your sacred wing.

Through you may we the Father know,
through you th' eternal Son,
and you the Spirit of them both,
thrice-blessed Three in One.

All glory to the Father be,
with his co-equal Son,
the same to you, great Paraclete,
while endless ages run.
Amen.

BIBLIOGRAPHY

Bucke, Richard M., *Cosmic Consciousness: A Study in the Evolution of the Human Mind.* Internet Sacred Text Archive, E.P. Dutton and Company, Inc., 1901, http://sacred-texts.com.

Burke, Abbot George (Swami Nirmalananda Giri), *The Christ of India: The Story of Original Christianity* (Light of the Spirit Press, Cedar Crest, NM, 2nd edition, 2018), Kindle edition.

Cady, H. Emilie, *Lessons in Truth.* Internet Sacred Text Archive, Lee Summit, MO, Unity School of Christianity, 1894, http://sacred-texts.com.

Cayce, Egar, *Edgar Cayce on Christ Consciousness.* https://www.edgarcayce.org/the-readings/spiritual-growth/christ-conciousness/.

Cross, Christina, *http://smilingsouls.com* (Linda Howe Center for Energy Integrity, 101 N. Marion St., Oak Park, IL 60303, 2001)

Durckheim, Karlfreid, *The Way of Transformation* (Harper Collins, Scranton, PA, 1980)

Foundation for Inner Peace, *A Course in Miracles* (Penguin Books USA Inc., New York, NY, 1975, most recent published revision 1996)

Funicelli, Pellegrino, *The Bible and Padre Pio* (Voice, vol. II, No. 4, 1972)

Ghezzi, Bert, *Mystics & Miracles* (Loyola Press, Chicago, IL 2002)

Hendricks, Gay, *Conscious Breathing* (Bantam Dell Publishing Group, 1995)

Hick, John, *God Has Many Names* (The Westminster Press, Philadelphia, PA, 1980, 1982)

Hoppe, Geoffrey and Tobias, *Twelve Signs of Your Awakening Divinity* (reprinted with permission, www.crimsoncircle.com)

John of the Cross, *Counsels of Light and Love* (Paulist Press, New York, 1978)

Koenig-Bricker, Woodeene, *Praying with the Saints: Making Their Prayers Your Own* (Loyola Press, Chicago, IL 2001)

Krishnananda, Swami, *The Mandukya Upanishad* (translation from The Divine Life Society, Rishikesh, India, http://www.swami-krishnananda.org)

Kriyananda, Goswami, *The Patanjali Yoga Sutras* (The Temple of Kriya Yoga, Chicago, IL, 1998)

Kriyananda, Goswami, *The Spiritual Science of Kriya Yoga* (The Temple of Kriya Yoga, Chicago, IL, 2002, first published 1976)

Melchizedek, Drunvalo, *The Ancient Secret of the Flower of Life: Volume I & Volume II* (Light Technology Publishing, Flagstaff, AZ, first printing 1990, last printing 1998)

Moss, Robert, *Dreamgates: Exploring the Worlds of Soul, Imagination, and Life Beyond Death* (Novato CA: New World Library, 2010)

Prophet, Elizabeth Clare, *Maitreya on the Image of God: A Study in Christhood by the Great Initiator* (Summit University Press, Corwin Springs, MT, 1990)

Prophet, Elizabeth Clare, *The Lost Years of Jesus* (Summit University Press, Corwin Springs, MT, 1987)

Ramasamy, MD;DPM; Dr. Annadurai Variankaval, (2019). "Aramaic words and Tamil (The language of Jesus)." Retrieved from http://www.Academia.edu

Ruffin, C. Bernard, *Padre Pio: The True Story* (Our Sunday Visitor, Inc., Huntington, IN, 1982)

Socrates, translation by Benjamin Jowett, *Phaedrus.* Internet Sacred Text Archive, C. Scribner's Sons, NY, 1871, http://sacred-texts.com.

Sivananda, Swami, *International Sivananda Yoga Vendanta Centres,* (www.Sivananda.org)

Underhill, Evelyn, "Mysticism: The Nature and Development of Spiritual Consciousness." *Internet Sacred Text Archive*, London, Methuen, 1911, http://sacred-texts.com.

Van Auken, John, *Personal Spirituality Newsletter* (Association for Research & Enlightenment, Virginia Beach, VA)

Webster, *Revised Unabridged Dictionary*, © 1996, 1998 MICRA, Inc.

White, John, *From Morality to Mysticism,* (What is Enlightenment?, Spring/Summer 2002, page 94)

Yogananda, Paramahansa, *Autobiography of a Yogi* (Self-Realization Fellowship, Los Angeles, CA, 1946)

Yogananda, Paramahansa, *The Second Coming of Christ* (Self-Realization Fellowship, Los Angeles, CA, 2004)

Made in the USA
San Bernardino, CA
16 January 2020